2017 SQA Past Papers with Answers

Higher

MODERN STUDIES

2015, 2016 & 2017 Exams

HODDER
GIBSON
AN HACHETTE UK COMPANY

Activity 2 – Use technology!

Why should everything be written down? Have you thought about "mental" maps, diagrams, cartoons and colour to help you learn? And rather than write down notes, why not record your revision material?

What about having a text message revision session with friends? Keep in touch with them to find out how and what they are revising and share ideas and questions.

Why not make a video diary where you tell the camera what you are doing, what you think you have learned and what you still have to do? No one has to see or hear it, but the process of having to organise your thoughts in a formal way to explain something is a very important learning practice.

Be sure to make use of electronic files. You could begin to summarise your class notes. Your typing might be slow, but it will get faster and the typed notes will be easier to read than the scribbles in your class notes. Try to add different fonts and colours to make your work stand out. You can easily Google relevant pictures, cartoons and diagrams which you can copy and paste to make your work more attractive and **MEMORABLE**.

Activity 3 – This is it. Do this and you will know lots!

Step 1

In this task you must be very honest with yourself! Find the SQA syllabus for your subject (www.sqa.org.uk). Look at how it is broken down into main topics called MANDATORY knowledge. That means stuff you MUST know.

Step 2

BEFORE you do ANY revision on this topic, write a list of everything that you already know about the subject. It might be quite a long list but you only need to write it once. It shows you all the information that is already in your long-term memory so you know what parts you do not need to revise!

Step 3

Pick a chapter or section from your book or revision notes. Choose a fairly large section or a whole chapter to get the most out of this activity.

With a buddy, use Skype, Facetime, Twitter or any other communication you have, to play the game "If this is the answer, what is the question?". For example, if you are revising Geography and the answer you provide is "meander", your buddy would have to make up a question like "What is the word that describes a feature of a river where it flows slowly and bends often from side to side?".

Make up 10 "answers" based on the content of the chapter or section you are using. Give this to your buddy to solve while you solve theirs.

Step 4

Construct a wordsearch of at least 10 × 10 squares. You can make it as big as you like but keep it realistic. Work together with a group of friends. Many apps allow you to make wordsearch puzzles online. The words and phrases can go in any direction and phrases can be split. Your puzzle must only contain facts linked to the topic you are revising. Your task is to find 10 bits of information to hide in your puzzle, but you must not repeat information that you used in Step 3. DO NOT show where the words are. Fill up empty squares with random letters. Remember to keep a note of where your answers are hidden but do not show your friends. When you have a complete puzzle, exchange it with a friend to solve each other's puzzle.

Step 5

Now make up 10 questions (not "answers" this time) based on the same chapter used in the previous two tasks. Again, you must find NEW information that you have not yet used. Now it's getting hard to find that new information! Again, give your questions to a friend to answer.

Step 6

As you have been doing the puzzles, your brain has been actively searching for new information. Now write a NEW LIST that contains only the new information you have discovered when doing the puzzles. Your new list is the one to look at repeatedly for short bursts over the next few days. Try to remember more and more of it without looking at it. After a few days, you should be able to add words from your second list to your first list as you increase the information in your long-term memory.

FINALLY! Be inspired...

Make a list of different revision ideas and beside each one write **THINGS I HAVE** tried, **THINGS I WILL** try and **THINGS I MIGHT** try. Don't be scared of trying something new.

And remember – "FAIL TO PREPARE AND PREPARE TO FAIL!"

Higher Modern Studies

The course

You will have studied the following three units:

- Democracy in Scotland and the United Kingdom
- Social Issues in the United Kingdom
- International Issues

Your teacher will usually have chosen one topic from each of the three sections above and you will answer questions on these in your exam (see table below).

Unit of the course	Option one	Option two
Democracy in Scotland and the UK	Democracy in Scotland	Democracy in the UK
Social Issues in the UK	Social Inequality	Crime and the Law
International Issues	World Powers	World Issues

Candidates are expected to complete three internal unit assessment items (part knowledge and understanding and part source-based). These must be completed to gain an overall course award.

The added value comes from the question paper and is an externally-marked assessment. This consists of two parts:

- Higher question paper

  60 marks allocated – two-thirds of marks
- Higher assignment

  30 marks allocated – one-third of marks

Total marks available = 90

The marks you achieve in the question paper and assignment are added together and an overall grade will be awarded. The grade is based on your total marks. Based on notional difficulty, 63 and above (70% and above) is an A; 54–62 (60%–69%) is a B; and 45–53 (50% to 59%) is a C.

The question paper

You will have 2 hours and 15 minutes to complete the question paper with a total of 60 marks allocated. There are three sections with each section worth 20 marks.

There are 16 marks available for skills-based questions and 44 marks for knowledge and understanding. These are assessed in three extended responses worth either 12 or 20 marks.

In the exam paper, more marks are awarded for knowledge and understanding than skills so it is crucial that you have a sound grasp of content.

Skills or source-based questions

There are two types of skills questions that you will have practised in class. Both are allocated 8 marks. These are:

1. Using up to three complex sources of information: **'to what extent is it accurate to state that…'**
2. Using up to three complex sources of information: **'what conclusions can be drawn…'**

As preparation for your exam, the best advice would be to practise source-based questions and to review the types of information required by an examiner for full marks. Remember, all the answers in source-based questions are contained within the sources. No marks are awarded for additional knowledge.

Knowledge (or extended response) questions

In the knowledge section of your exam you could be asked questions that have a similar style to the following:

- **Discuss – 20-mark extended response**, for example:

  The political system provides an effective check on the government.

  Discuss with reference to a world power you have studied.
- **To what extent – 20-mark extended response**, for example:

  To what extent has a world issue you have studied had an impact in different countries?
- **Evaluate – 12-mark extended response**, for example:

  One aim of an electoral system is to provide fair representation.

  Evaluate the effectiveness of an electoral system you have studied in providing fair representation.

  You should refer to electoral systems used in Scotland or the United Kingdom or both in your answer.
- **Analyse – 12-mark extended response**, for example:

  Analyse the different lifestyle choices that may result in poor health.

Remember, in your course exam the knowledge questions for the International Issues section will not refer to a particular country or issue. You will be expected to base your answer around your knowledge and understanding of the World Power or World Issue you have studied.

Remember, also, in your course exam the two skills-based questions may appear in any two of the three sections. There will be no choice offered for skills-based questions. For example, if a skills-based question is examined in the Social Issues section, it will either be based on Social Inequality or Crime and the Law. The question is testing your skills and no knowledge is needed to answer the question.

What makes a good extended response answer?

- One that answers the question and only provides knowledge and understanding and analysis/evaluation that is **relevant** to the question.

- One that is aware of the different requirements of a 20-mark and 12-mark answer. A 20-mark answer should include greater skills of analysis and evaluation and be more structured than a 12-mark answer.

- One that uses **up-to-date, relevant** examples to illustrate your understanding of the question being asked.

- One that includes a range of points with detailed exemplification and explanation, and analysis/evaluation.

- For a 12-mark answer, one that includes knowledge/understanding and **either** analysis **or** evaluation. For a 20-mark response, one that includes knowledge/understanding, analysis, evaluation, a structure/line of argument and draws valid conclusions that address the question.

What makes a poor extended response answer?

- One that does not answer the question, or tries to change the question being asked. This is sometimes called "turning a question".

- One that gives detailed description or explanation that is not relevant to the question.

- One that contains information which is out of date.

- One that **only** provides a list of facts with no development or analysis/evaluation.

What makes a poor source-based answer?

- One that doesn't make use of all of the sources provided.

- One that fails to link information across sources.

- For the "objectivity" question, one that fails to make an overall judgement on the statement or fails to comment on the validity or reliability of the sources.

- For the "conclusions" question, one that fails to make an overall conclusion.

So you are now ready to answer the exam questions. Keep calm and don't panic.

Good luck!

HIGHER

2015

National Qualifications 2015

X749/76/11

Modern Studies

WEDNESDAY, 27 MAY

9:00 AM – 11:15 AM

Total marks — 60

SECTION 1 — DEMOCRACY IN SCOTLAND AND THE UNITED KINGDOM — 20 marks

Attempt **EITHER** Question 1(a) **OR** 1(b)

SECTION 2 — SOCIAL ISSUES IN THE UNITED KINGDOM — 20 marks
　　　　Part A Social inequality in the United Kingdom
　　　　Part B Crime and the law in the United Kingdom

Attempt Question 2 and **EITHER** Question 3(a) **OR** 3(b) **OR** 3(c) **OR** 3(d)

SECTION 3 — INTERNATIONAL ISSUES — 20 marks
　　　　Part A World Powers
　　　　Part B World Issues

Attempt Question 4 and **EITHER** Question 5(a) **OR** 5(b) **OR** 5(c) **OR** 5(d)

Write your answers clearly in the answer booklet provided. In the answer booklet, you must clearly identify the question number you are attempting.

Use **blue** or **black** ink.

Before leaving the examination room you must give your answer booklet to the Invigilator; if you do not, you may lose all the marks for this paper.

MARKS

SECTION 1 — DEMOCRACY IN SCOTLAND AND THE UNITED KINGDOM — 20 marks

Attempt **EITHER** Question 1(a) **OR** 1(b)

Question 1

(a)

Some factors are more important than others in influencing voting behaviour.

To what extent are some factors more important than others in influencing voting behaviour?

You should refer to voting behaviour in Scotland **or** the United Kingdom **or** both in your answer.

20

OR

(b)

Most citizens participate effectively in the political process.

Discuss.

You should refer to participation in Scotland **or** the United Kingdom **or** both in your answer.

20

[Turn over for SECTION 2 on *Page four*]

DO NOT WRITE ON THIS PAGE

SECTION 2 — SOCIAL ISSUES IN THE UNITED KINGDOM — 20 marks

Attempt Question 2 and **EITHER** Question 3(a) **OR** 3(b) **OR** 3(c) **OR** 3(d)

Question 2

Study Sources A, B and C then attempt the question which follows.

SOURCE A

Reducing smoking remains a challenge

Despite the ban on smoking in enclosed public places which came into force in 2006, smoking still accounts for more than 13,000 deaths in Scotland each year and is the main cause of early death. Treating people with smoking related conditions costs NHS Scotland about £271 million each year. Smoking in young people can lead to addiction and damage to their hearts and lungs. Almost 600 children — some as young as 11 — take up smoking every day across the UK. Figures from Cancer Research UK estimate that 463 children start smoking every day in England, 50 in Scotland, 30 in Wales and 19 in Northern Ireland. These habits, if continued into adulthood, can lead to further ill health and can affect a person's ability to work.

Tobacco has financial costs as well as health costs for young smokers, with a pack of 20 cigarettes costing around £8. Survey data from Scotland shows that 17% of both 13 and 15 year old regular smokers i.e. those who smoke at least once per week, spend more than £20 per week on cigarettes. In Scotland, 39% of those in the most deprived areas smoke, compared to just 10% in the least deprived areas.

The government has introduced legislation aimed at reducing the number of people who take up smoking. This includes changes to the ways cigarettes can be displayed in supermarkets, removing cigarette vending machines from pubs and raising the age to buy cigarettes to 18 years.

The Scottish Government has also proposed other policies to reduce smoking, aiming for Scotland to be tobacco free by 2034. Before then, plans include the introduction of plain packaging, smoke free hospital grounds and additional funding for education programmes which try to stop young people from taking up smoking in the first place.

In 2013, less than one quarter of Scottish adults smoked. This continues a downward trend in this figure. Smoking rates differ depending where you live in the UK. Scotland reported the highest proportion of current smokers with 23%. This compared to 19% in England, 21% in Wales and 19% in Northern Ireland. However, those groups who are out of work and rely on benefits for their income remain the most likely groups to smoke.

Source: Adapted from bbc.co.uk (March 2013) and Cancer Research UK

SOURCE B — Percentage (%) who smoke in Scotland by economic status* (2012)   MARKS

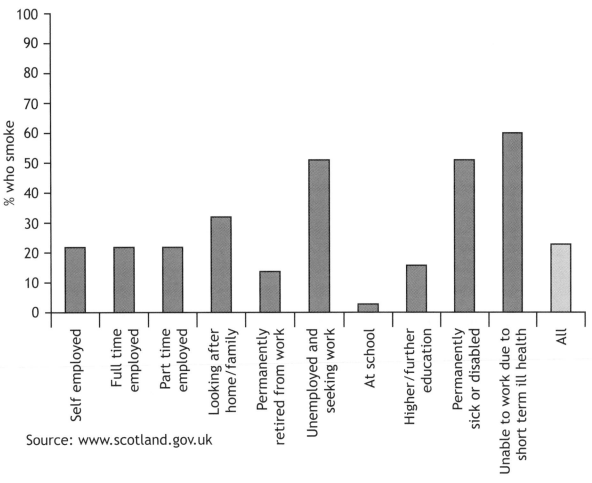

Source: www.scotland.gov.uk

*Note: Economic status refers to the ways people earn their income, for example from earnings if working or through Social Security benefits if unemployed or disabled.

SOURCE C — Percentage (%) of 13 and 15 year olds who smoke regularly 1990-2013 and 2014-2018 (projected)

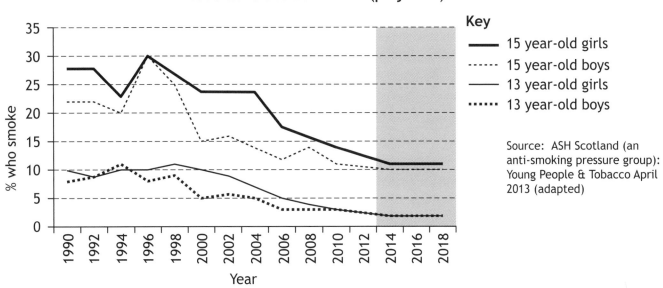

Key
— 15 year-old girls
···· 15 year-old boys
— 13 year-old girls
▪▪▪▪ 13 year-old boys

Source: ASH Scotland (an anti-smoking pressure group): Young People & Tobacco April 2013 (adapted)

Attempt the following question, using **only** the information in Sources A, B and C opposite and above.

To what extent is it accurate to state that the government's policies are successfully tackling the problem of smoking in Scotland?   **8**

MARKS

Attempt **EITHER** Question 3(a) **OR** 3(b) **OR** 3(c) **OR** 3(d)

Question 3

Part A: Social inequality in the United Kingdom

Answers may refer to Scotland **or** the United Kingdom **or** both.

(a) Evaluate the view that social inequality affects some groups in society more than others.

12

OR

(b) Evaluate the effectiveness of **either** the benefits system **or** health services in tackling social inequality.

12

OR

Part B: Crime and the law in the United Kingdom

Answers may refer to Scotland **or** the United Kingdom **or** both.

(c) Evaluate the view that crime only affects the victims.

12

OR

(d) Evaluate the effectiveness of **either** prison sentences **or** community based sentences in tackling crime.

12

[Turn over for SECTION 3 on *Page eight*]

DO NOT WRITE ON THIS PAGE

SECTION 3 — INTERNATIONAL ISSUES — 20 marks

Attempt Question 4 and **EITHER** Question 5(a) **OR** 5(b) **OR** 5(c) **OR** 5(d)

Question 4

Study Sources A, B and C then attempt the question which follows.

SOURCE A

The Recession and The Eurozone

When the Euro launched in 1999 it became the official currency of 11 European Union (EU) member countries. Gradually, more countries saw the Euro's benefits and adopted it as their currency. Today over 336 million people in 19 countries use it and form what we call the Eurozone. Nine EU countries have not joined the Eurozone.

During the recession which began in 2008, the Euro struggled to compete against stronger currencies such as the dollar which led to some countries reporting a series of long term economic problems.

As a result of the recession, across the EU, many businesses lost sales and cut jobs. The unemployment rate throughout the EU went from 7% in 2008 to 10% in 2014 with an estimated 24·5 million people out of work.

Some Eurozone members have required financial hand-outs to help them cope with their growing level of debt. In May 2010 Greece received 110 billion Euros followed by 130 billion Euros in 2012. Ireland and Spain have also benefited from a 90 billion Euro hand-out. Portugal received financial assistance twice within the space of a year. However, some Eurozone countries such as Germany have benefited from using the Euro to build up trade and generate income, which has kept their debt levels comparatively low. In the EU, debt went from 63% of Gross Domestic Product* (GDP) in 2008 to 89% of GDP in 2014.

Largely because of an increase in part time jobs, the UK's economy has not suffered as badly as some other Non-Eurozone members in terms of unemployment. Some other Non-Eurozone countries have not seen big increases in unemployment as many of their young people have moved to other countries in order to find work.

The Eurozone is a huge market for businesses from the United States, China, India, Japan, Russia and other major world economic powers who have been affected by the recession despite not being EU members. In 2008 these five powers purchased 41% of EU exports. By 2014 this figure was 37%. The collapse of the Euro or a situation where countries are unable to repay their debt could trigger a further world-wide recession.

*Gross Domestic Product – total value of goods and services produced in one country

---

SOURCE B   MARKS

Unemployment Rates (%) — Selected Eurozone members

Country	(2008)	(2014)
Ireland	6·4	11
Greece	7·7	25·9
Portugal	8·5	15·3
Spain	11·3	25·6
Cyprus	3·7	15·3

Government Debt — Selected Eurozone members
(National debt as a percentage of GDP)

Country	(2008)	(2014)
Ireland	25%	123%
Greece	105%	175%
Portugal	68%	129%
Spain	36%	72%
Cyprus	59%	112%

SOURCE C

Unemployment Rates (%) — Selected Non-Eurozone members

Country	(2008)	(2014)
UK	5·6	6
Sweden	6·2	8·1
Denmark	3·5	7
Poland	7·1	9·2
Romania	5·8	7·2

Government Debt — Selected Non-Eurozone members
(National debt as a percentage of GDP)

Country	(2008)	(2014)
UK	44%	90%
Sweden	40%	40%
Denmark	27%	44%
Poland	45%	57%
Romania	13%	38%

Attempt the following question, using **only** the information in Sources A, B and C opposite and above.

What conclusions can be drawn about the impact of the recession on different EU members?

You must draw conclusions about:

- the impact of the recession on Eurozone members
- the impact of the recession on Non-Eurozone members

You must now give an overall conclusion about the impact of the recession on the EU.   **8**

MARKS

Section 3 (continued)

Attempt **EITHER** Question 5(a) **OR** 5(b) **OR** 5(c) **OR** 5(d)

Question 5

Part A: World Powers

With reference to a world power you have studied:

(a) Analyse the ability of this world power to influence other countries.   **12**

OR

(b) Analyse the impact of a recent social issue on this world power.   **12**

OR

Part B: World Issues

With reference to a world issue you have studied:

(c) Analyse the role of international organisations in attempting to resolve this issue.   **12**

OR

(d) Analyse the different factors which have caused this issue.   **12**

[END OF QUESTION PAPER]

HIGHER

2016

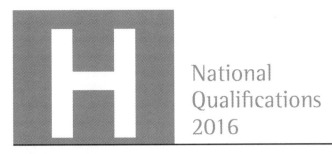

National Qualifications 2016

X749/76/11

Modern Studies

MONDAY, 30 MAY

9:00 AM — 11:15 AM

Total marks — 60

SECTION 1 — DEMOCRACY IN SCOTLAND AND THE UNITED KINGDOM — 20 marks

Attempt Question 1 and **EITHER** Question 2(a) **OR** 2(b)

SECTION 2 — SOCIAL ISSUES IN THE UNITED KINGDOM — 20 marks
Part A Social inequality in the United Kingdom
Part B Crime and the law in the United Kingdom

Attempt **EITHER** Question 3(a) **OR** 3(b) **OR** 3(c) **OR** 3(d)

SECTION 3 — INTERNATIONAL ISSUES — 20 marks
Part A World Powers
Part B World Issues

Attempt Question 4 and **EITHER** Question 5(a) **OR** 5(b) **OR** 5(c) **OR** 5(d)

Write your answers clearly in the answer booklet provided. In the answer booklet you must clearly identify the question number you are attempting.

Use **blue** or **black** ink.

Before leaving the examination room you must give your answer booklet to the Invigilator; if you do not, you may lose all the marks for this paper.

SECTION 1 — DEMOCRACY IN SCOTLAND AND THE UNITED KINGDOM — 20 marks

Attempt Question 1 and **EITHER** Question 2(a) **OR** 2(b)

Question 1

Study Sources A, B and C then attempt the question which follows.

SOURCE A

Political Inequality in the UK and why Voting Matters

A central claim of democracy is that every citizen's preference, no matter what their socio-economic status, should count equally. There are, however, good reasons for supposing that the principle of political equality and democracy are under threat and that politics is increasingly becoming the preserve of the rich and the powerful. In Britain, there is a growing public belief that some groups in the British population are better represented politically than others. There is a widespread suspicion that governments are more likely to pass laws which benefit the groups most likely to vote.

A great problem facing British democracy is the growing inequality within voter turnout. Although overall turnout was 66·1% in 2015, electoral participation is lower among lower income groups, mainly Social Classes D and E. This gives better-off voters, mainly in Social Classes A and B, disproportionate influence at the ballot box.

Unequal turnout reinforces a vicious cycle of disaffection and under-representation among those groups where electoral participation is falling. As government policy becomes less responsive to their interests the less inclined they will be to vote. The less they vote, the less likely governments will respond to their interests; thus establishing a downward spiral excluding poorer socio-economic groups from electoral life.

Those who vote at their first eligible election are considerably more likely to vote throughout the duration of their life. Forcing young people to turnout at the ballot box is one option that might break the non-voting habit plaguing our youth and would have a substantial impact on voter turnout as each generation ages. However, Scotland managed to engage its younger generation during the 2014 Independence Referendum without compulsory voting. The subsequent 7% increase in Scottish turnout at the 2015 General Election was largely responsible for the small increase in turnout across the whole UK.

SOURCE B
UK General Election Statistics

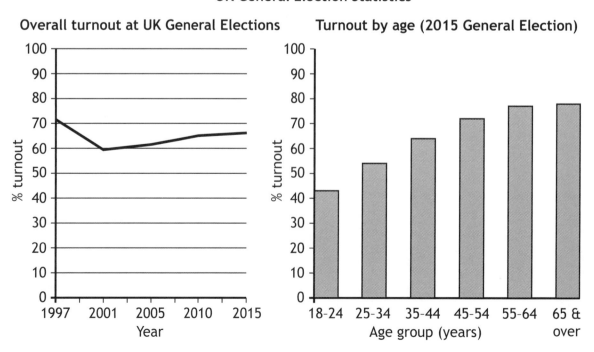

Overall turnout at UK General Elections

Turnout by age (2015 General Election)

Source B (continued)

Turnout by Social Class (2015 General Election)   Turnout by Housing type (2015 General Election)

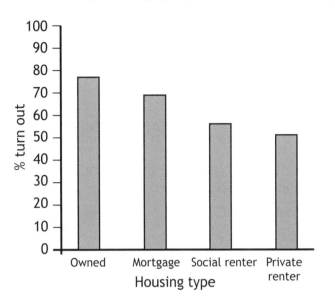

SOURCE C

Selected Government Policies (Introduced between the 2010 and 2015 General Elections)

Policy	Description
VAT increased to 20%	Disproportionately affected poorest households more than middle to upper income levels
End of Educational Maintenance Allowance (EMA) in England and Wales	Removal of Government financial aid to help pupils from poorer backgrounds to stay on at school
Child Tax Credit	Households earning more than £40,000 per year will not receive this
Cap on Benefits	Households in receipt of benefits will receive no more than average UK family income
Bedroom Tax	Removal of some benefit for those staying in rented housing that has excess bedroom capacity
Flat Rate State Pension/ Retirement Age	Increase from £97 per week to £140 for single pensioners and an increase in retirement age to 68
Child Benefit means tested	Those earning over £50,000 will no longer receive this benefit
Housing Benefit	Under 26s no longer allowed to claim this benefit
Top Rate Tax Cut	5% reduction in tax levels for those earning more than £150,000 per year

Attempt the following question, using **only** the information in Sources A, B and C on *Page two and above*.

What conclusions can be drawn about turnout in the UK?

You **must** draw **one** conclusion about each of the following;

- the link between government policy and the turnout of different age groups
- the link between government policy and the turnout of different socio-economic groups

You **must** give an overall conclusion about turnout in the UK.   **8**

MARKS

Section 1 (continued)

Attempt **EITHER** Question 2(a) **OR** 2(b)

Question 2

(a)

Electoral systems allow the views of the electorate to be represented.

Analyse the ways in which an electoral system you have studied allows the views of the electorate to be represented.

You should refer to an electoral system used in Scotland **or** the United Kingdom **or** both in your answer.

12

OR

(b)

Individuals and groups in society can influence government decision making in many ways.

Analyse the ways in which individuals and groups in society can influence government decision making.

You should refer to individuals and groups in Scotland **or** the United Kingdom **or** both in your answer.

12

MARKS

SECTION 2 - SOCIAL ISSUES IN THE UNITED KINGDOM - 20 marks

Attempt **EITHER** question 3(a) **OR** 3(b) **OR** 3(c) **OR** 3(d)

Question 3

Part A: Social inequality in the United Kingdom

Answers may refer to Scotland **or** the United Kingdom **or** both.

(a) Government policies have failed to reduce social inequalities.
Discuss.   **20**

OR

(b) To what extent can ill-health be blamed on the lifestyle choices of the population?   **20**

OR

Part B: Crime and the law in the United Kingdom

Answers may refer to Scotland **or** the United Kingdom **or** both.

(c) Government policies have failed to reduce crime.
Discuss.   **20**

OR

(d) To what extent is human nature the main cause of crime?   **20**

[Turn over

SECTION 3 — INTERNATIONAL ISSUES — 20 marks

Attempt Question 4 and **EITHER** Question 5(a) **OR** 5(b) **OR** 5(c) **OR** 5(d)

Question 4

Study Sources A, B and C then attempt the question which follows.

SOURCE A

Russia's "Foreign Agents"

In 2012 Russia's parliament adopted a law that required campaign groups to register as "foreign agents" with the Ministry of Justice if they engaged in "political activity" and received foreign funding. The definition of "political activity" under the law is so broad and vague that it covered almost all campaign groups in Russia.

Russian authorities arrested and harassed activists, blocked independent online media and proposed measures that would further stifle free expression. More recently pro-government media published material blaming the government of Ukraine for the on-going civil war in that country, trying to deflect attention away from Russia's invasion and occupation of Crimea.

In Russia "foreign agent" is interpreted as "spy" or "traitor." The groups campaigning for political freedoms were in no doubt that the law aimed to demonise them, and to turn the public against them. Russia's many human rights groups boycotted the law, calling it "slanderous." Many of them have now been forced to disband and many of their leaders have been prosecuted for refusing to register as a "foreign agent". In the past such individuals may have faced the death sentence but Russia has not executed anyone since 1996.

In August 2013, four organisations challenged the law in Russia's Constitutional Court. On April 8, 2014 the court upheld the law, ruling that the term "foreign agent" had no negative connotations, therefore, its use was "not intended to persecute or discredit" anyone. The court also found that labelling campaign groups as "foreign agents" was in the interests of state security and did not affect the right to protest. The ruling has been heavily criticised by many foreign governments.

Source: Adapted from the website of an international pressure group campaigning to improve human rights.

SOURCE B

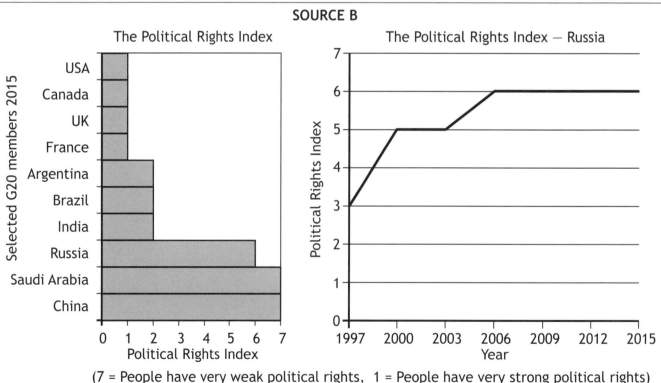

The Political Rights Index

The Political Rights Index — Russia

(7 = People have very weak political rights, 1 = People have very strong political rights)

Source: Adapted from an academic website for students and teachers of international affairs.

Note: The Political Rights Index measures how free and fair elections are, the right to free speech and to campaign, and the fairness of government departments including the police, courts and prisons.

MARKS

SOURCE C

Annual Report 2014

"There have been fewer complaints from Russians over human rights violations", Government spokesman Vladimir Lukin said in his annual report. He said that more than half of the complaints he had received last year were about violations of civil rights and freedoms. The number of complaints concerning political rights was relatively small, and complaints about religious freedoms and freedom of conscience decreased by 10%.

In 2014, Mr Lukin's offices received 24,000 complaints; in 2012 the figure was 58,000. Many people were worried about violations of their personal rights, others complained about unfair court rulings; more than half of the letters (56%) were complaints about the courts and nearly one-quarter of the complaints were about abuses by the police or prison staff. As for political complaints, they accounted for 2% of the total. Lukin also praised a recent report by the European Union which congratulated Russia on its expansion of jury trials right across Russia and its suspension of the death penalty.

As he submitted his report to President Vladimir Putin, Lukin brought up the issue of mass inspections of human rights groups, launched in recent weeks. Lukin assured the journalists that political campaign groups had nothing to fear and that their right to protest was protected by Russian law.

Source: Adapted from the website of the Russian Government's news agency.

Attempt the following question, using **only** the information in Sources A, B and C on *Page six* and above.

To what extent is it accurate to state that Russia effectively protects the rights of its citizens?

In your answer, you may wish to evaluate the reliability of the sources.

8

[Turn over for next question

MARKS

Section 3 (continued)

Attempt **EITHER** Question 5(a) **OR** 5(b) **OR** 5(c) **OR** 5(d)

Part A: World Powers

With reference to a world power you have studied:

(a) Evaluate the success of the Government in tackling a socio-economic issue.   **12**

OR

(b) Evaluate the effectiveness of the political system in representing the wishes of the population.   **12**

OR

Part B: World Issues

With reference to a world issue you have studied:

(c) Evaluate the impact of this issue on the individuals and groups affected.   **12**

OR

(d) Evaluate the effectiveness of international organisations in addressing this issue.   **12**

[END OF QUESTION PAPER]

HIGHER

2017

National Qualifications 2017

X749/76/11

Modern Studies

FRIDAY, 19 MAY

9:00 AM – 11:15 AM

Total marks — 60

SECTION 1 — DEMOCRACY IN SCOTLAND AND THE UNITED KINGDOM — 20 marks

Attempt **EITHER** Question 1(a) **OR** 1(b) **AND** Question 2

SECTION 2 — SOCIAL ISSUES IN THE UNITED KINGDOM — 20 marks

Part A Social inequality in the United Kingdom

Part B Crime and the law in the United Kingdom

Attempt **EITHER** Question 3(a) **OR** 3(b) **OR** 3(c) **OR** 3(d)

SECTION 3 — INTERNATIONAL ISSUES — 20 marks

Part A World Powers

Part B World Issues

Attempt **EITHER** Question 4(a) **OR** 4(b) **OR** 4(c) **OR** 4(d) **AND** Question 5

Write your answers clearly in the answer booklet provided. In the answer booklet you must clearly identify the question number you are attempting.

Use **blue** or **black** ink.

Before leaving the examination room you must give your answer booklet to the Invigilator; if you do not, you may lose all the marks for this paper.

MARKS

SECTION 1 — DEMOCRACY IN SCOTLAND AND THE UNITED KINGDOM — 20 marks

Attempt **EITHER** Question 1 (a) **OR** Question 1 (b) **AND** Question 2

Question 1

(a)

Voting systems aim to provide fair representation.

Evaluate the effectiveness of **one** voting system you have studied in providing fair representation.

You should refer to Scotland **or** the United Kingdom **or** both in your answer.

12

OR

(b)

One role of Parliament is to hold the Government to account.

Evaluate the effectiveness of Parliament in holding the Government to account.

You should refer to Scotland **or** the United Kingdom **or** both in your answer.

12

[Turn over for next question

DO NOT WRITE ON THIS PAGE

Question 2

Study Sources A, B and C then attempt the question which follows.

SOURCE A

Scottish Independence Referendum

The Scottish Independence Referendum was notable for several reasons. First of all it gave the vote to 16 and 17 year olds for the first time. Also because, if successful, it would have led to the breakup of the 300 year old United Kingdom. Finally, it was notable for the high level of political debate and interest within Scotland during the campaign.

Across all 32 council areas in Scotland, 85% of voters participated and when all of the votes had been counted, the result was clear: Scotland had chosen to remain part of the United Kingdom by a margin of 55% to 45%. Over 3·6 million votes were cast. Just over 2 million voters chose to place their "X" in the "NO" box in responding to the question "Should Scotland be an Independent Country?".

In the days and weeks that followed, political scientists tried to provide reasons why people voted the way they did. Although the average turnout was 85%, this figure varied greatly between areas with different socio-economic profiles. Of the 32 Scottish council areas, 4 voted YES. What is striking is that each of these 4 areas had high levels of poverty and social deprivation.

The influence of age as a factor was considered by many, particularly as 16 and 17 year olds were allowed to vote. However, it may have been the decisions of older voters rather than their younger counterparts that were important, particularly as older voters are more likely to turn out in higher numbers. Female voters seemed to be swayed more by the NO campaign's arguments.

Result and Turnout
Scottish Independence Referendum (Selected Regions)

Region	Yes (%)	Turnout (%)
Aberdeen City	41·4	81·7
Aberdeenshire	39·6	87·2
Dundee City	57·4	78·8
East Dunbartonshire	38·8	91
East Renfrewshire	36·8	90·4
Edinburgh	38·9	84·4
Glasgow	53·5	75
North Lanarkshire	51·1	84·4
Perth and Kinross	39·8	86·9
West Dunbartonshire	54	87·9

SOURCE B

How Did You Vote in the Referendum?

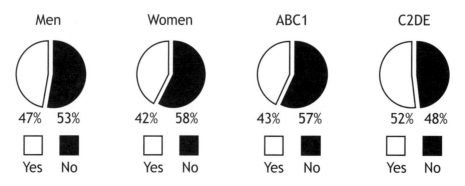

Men	Women	ABC1	C2DE
47% 53%	42% 58%	43% 57%	52% 48%
Yes No	Yes No	Yes No	Yes No

MARKS

Question 2 Source B (continued)

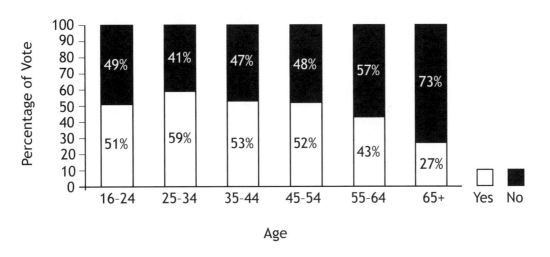

SOURCE C

Social and Economic Indicators (Selected Regions)

	% Employment Rate	% Unemployment Rate	% of Child Poverty in Region
Aberdeen City	77·3	1·4	18
Aberdeenshire	78·6	0·6	14
Dundee City	61·4	4·4	28
East Dunbartonshire	77·1	1·4	13
East Renfrewshire	74·2	1·4	15
Edinburgh	71·7	2·2	21
Glasgow	63·3	4·2	33
North Lanarkshire	70·2	3·8	25
Perth and Kinross	75·3	1·6	17
West Dunbartonshire	65·2	4·3	25

Attempt the following question, using **only** the information in Sources A, B and C on *Page four and above*.

What conclusions can be drawn about the result of the Scottish Independence Referendum?

You must draw conclusions about:

- the influence of poverty and social deprivation on voting behaviour
- the influence of age on voting behaviour

You should provide an overall conclusion on the most important factors influencing the result of the Scottish Independence Referendum.

8

SECTION 2 — SOCIAL ISSUES IN THE UNITED KINGDOM — 20 marks

Attempt **EITHER** question 3 (a) **OR** 3 (b) **OR** 3 (c) **OR** 3 (d)

Question 3

Part A: Social inequality in the United Kingdom

Answers may refer to Scotland **or** the United Kingdom **or** both.

(a)   Poverty is the main cause of poor health.

Discuss.   **20**

OR

(b)   To what extent have government policies been effective in reducing social and economic inequalities?   **20**

OR

Part B: Crime and the law in the United Kingdom

Answers may refer to Scotland **or** the United Kingdom **or** both.

(c)   Poverty is the main cause of crime.

Discuss.   **20**

OR

(d)   To what extent have prisons failed to meet their aims?   **20**

MARKS

SECTION 3 — INTERNATIONAL ISSUES — 20 marks

Attempt **EITHER** Question 4 (a) **OR** 4 (b) **OR** 4 (c) **OR** 4 (d) **AND** Question 5

Question 4

Part A: World Powers

With reference to a world power you have studied:

(a) Analyse the effects of a socio-economic issue on its people.   **12**

OR

(b) Analyse the different political opportunities that exist for people to influence decision making.   **12**

OR

Part B: World Issues

With reference to a world issue you have studied:

(c) Analyse the difficulties faced by those trying to resolve the issue.   **12**

OR

(d) Analyse the effects of the world issue on countries and their governments.   **12**

[Turn over

Question 5

Study Sources A, B and C then attempt the question which follows.

SOURCE A

Saudi Arabia: First women councillors elected

Women have been elected to local councils in Saudi Arabia for the first time after a ban on women taking part in elections was lifted. At least four women were elected, the state-run Saudi Press Agency (SPA) reported. Other news agencies put the number between 9 and 17. The vote is being seen as a landmark in the conservative kingdom. However, the local councils have limited powers.

Saudi women still face many curbs in public life, including driving. Officials said about 130,000 women had registered to vote in the poll, compared with 1·35 million men. The disparity was attributed by female voters to bureaucratic obstacles and a lack of transport. Female candidates were also not allowed to address male voters directly during campaigning. Turnout was high, state media reported. There were 2100 council seats available in the vote. An additional 1050 seats are appointed with approval from the King.

Salma bint Hizab al-Oteibi was named as Saudi Arabia's first elected female politician, after winning a seat on a local council. She was running against seven men and two women, the electoral authorities said.

Adapted from BBC News, 12/12/15

SOURCE B

Saudi Arabia: Selected Statistics

	Men	Women
Adult unemployment rate — 2015 (%)	2·7	20·8
University enrolment — 2015 (%)	56	59
Literacy rate — 2015 (%)	97	91
Allowed to drive — 2016	yes	no
Allowed to vote in local council elections — 2015	yes	yes
Earned income — 2015 (US dollars)	40000	17745
Shura Council Members — 2016	120	30
Percentage of the population 2015 (%)	57·5	42·5
Life expectancy — 2015 (years)	73	77
Candidates in 2015 local elections	5938	978
Seats won in 2015 local elections (%)	99·2	0·8

Source: Various Websites

MARKS

Question 5 (continued)

SOURCE C

Women Today in Saudi Arabia

A few Saudi women have risen to the top of the medical profession; for example, Dr. Ghada Al-Mutairi heads a medical research center in California and Dr. Salwa Al-Hazzaa is head of the ophthalmology department at King Faisal Specialist Hospital in Riyadh and was the late King Fahad's personal ophthalmologist.

In August 2013, a law was passed which made domestic violence against women illegal. The law carries penalties of up to 12 months in jail and a fine of 50,000 riyals ($13,000). However, convictions under this law are very rare. In Saudi courts the testimony of one man equals that of two women in family and inheritance law.

Elections of any kind are rare in Saudi Arabia and the recent election was only the third time in history that Saudis had gone to the polls. There were no elections at all between 1965 and 2005. The decision to allow women to take part in recent elections was taken by the late King Abdullah and is seen as a key part of his legacy. In announcing the reforms, King Abdullah said women in Saudi Arabia "have demonstrated positions that expressed correct opinions and advice".

Although Saudi Arabia imposes a strict dress code on women throughout the country, female newsreaders working for Al-Arabia news network which is partly owned by the son of the late King Fahad, are encouraged to adopt a Western dress code.

Before King Abdullah died in January 2015, he appointed 30 women to the country's Consultative Assembly, the Shura Council. But seats alone don't guarantee rights. Saudi Arabia's Consultative Assembly can propose laws, but ultimately only the king has the power to pass them.

Adapted from Wikipedia, 2016

Answer the following question, using **only** the information in Sources A, B and C on *Page eight* and above.

To what extent is it accurate to state that women now have greater political influence in Saudi Arabia?

In your answer, you may wish to evaluate the reliability of the sources.

8

[END OF QUESTION PAPER]

Page ten

[BLANK PAGE]

DO NOT WRITE ON THIS PAGE

Answers

General Marking Principles for Higher Modern Studies

Marking principles for each question type

For each of the question types the following provides an overview of marking principles.

The types of questions used in this paper are:
- Discuss ... [20 marks extended response]
- To what extent ... [20 marks extended response]
- Evaluate ... [12 marks extended response]
- Analyse ... [12 marks extended response]
- To what extent is it accurate to state that ... [information-handling question — 8 marks]
- What conclusions can be drawn ... [information-handling question — 8 marks]

Extended response (12 or 20 marks)

For 12 marks responses, up to a maximum of **8 marks** will be awarded for knowledge and understanding (description, explanation and exemplification). The remaining marks will be awarded for the demonstration of higher-order skills of analysis or evaluation. Where a candidate makes more analytical/evaluative points than are required to gain the maximum allocation of **4 marks**, these can be credited as knowledge and understanding marks provided they meet the criteria for this.

For 20 marks responses, up to **8 marks** will be awarded for knowledge and understanding (description, explanation and exemplification). The remaining marks will be awarded for the demonstration of higher-order skills of analysis and evaluation and structured argument. Where a candidate makes more analytical/evaluative points than are required to gain the maximum allocation of marks, these can be credited as knowledge and understanding marks provided they meet the criteria for this.

In the *Democracy in Scotland and the United Kingdom* and the *Social Issues in the United Kingdom* sections, candidates should be credited for responses which refer to Scotland only, to the United Kingdom only, or to both Scotland and the United Kingdom in their responses.

Analyse questions
- Candidates will identify parts of an issue, the relationship between these parts and their relationships with the whole; draw out and relate implications.

Evaluate questions
- Candidates will make a judgement based on criteria; determine the value of something.

Discuss questions
- Candidates will communicate ideas and information on the issue in the statement. Candidates will be credited for analysing and evaluating different views of the statement/viewpoint.

To what extent questions
- Candidates will analyse the issue in the question and come to a conclusion or conclusions which involve an evaluative judgement which is likely to be quantitative in nature.

Source-based questions that assess information-handling skills (8 marks)
- Questions will have at least two sources at an appropriate SCQF level.
- Award up to **3 marks** for a single developed point depending on the use of the evidence in the sources and the quality of the analysis/evaluation.
- Credit candidates who synthesise information both within and between sources.
- For **full marks** candidates must refer to all sources in their answer.

'Objectivity' questions
- For **full marks** candidates must make an overall judgement as to the extent of the accuracy of the given statement. Maximum 6 marks if no overall judgement is made on extent of accuracy of the statement.
- Credit may be given up to **2 marks** for answers which evaluate the usefulness or reliability of the source; however this is not required for **full marks**.

'Conclusions' questions
- For **full marks** candidates must make conclusions/judgements based upon evidence relating to the specific prompts in the question.
- Candidates are also required to make an overall conclusion about the issue in the question.

Higher Modern Studies marking grid for 12 marks questions (KU = 8 marks; analysis/evaluation = 4 marks)

	1 mark	2 marks	3 marks	4 marks
Range of relevant knowledge Accurate, relevant, up-to-date	One relevant aspect of the issue given with some description	Two relevant aspects of the issue given with some description or one relevant aspect covered with detailed and accurate description	One relevant aspect of issue with detailed and accurate description **and** one relevant aspect with some description	At least two relevant aspects with detailed and accurate descriptions – these should include the key aspects of the issue
Quality of explanation/ exemplification of knowledge Up to a maximum of **8 marks** available for knowledge and understanding	Some explanation of one aspect of the issue **or** relevant exemplification	Some explanation of two relevant aspects of the issue **or** detailed explanation of one aspect of the question which may include relevant exemplification	Detailed explanation of one relevant aspect of the issue with relevant exemplification **and** some explanation of one aspect of the question	At least two aspects of the question, fully explained, which relate closely to the key aspects of the question **and** extended, relevant, accurate and up-to-date exemplification
Analysis/evaluation Comments that identify relationships/ implications/make judgements **4 marks***	One relevant and accurate analytical or evaluative comment	One relevant and accurate analytical or evaluative comment that is justified **or** exemplified **or** two different relevant and accurate analytical/evaluative comments	One developed relevant and accurate analytical or evaluative comment that is justified **and** exemplified – this should relate closely to a key aspect of the question	One extended, accurate and justified analytical or evaluative comment of an insightful nature which relates closely to the key aspects of the question and is exemplified

*Where a candidate makes more analytical/evaluative points than are required to gain the maximum allocation of **4 marks**, these can be credited as knowledge and understanding marks provided they meet the criteria for this.

Answers to **12 marks** questions should demonstrate at least two relevant aspects of knowledge.

For full **marks** (12/12), a response must include a range of points, have detailed description/explanation, include a range of accurate exemplification and analysis or evaluation.

For full **marks** in the KU aspect of the question (8 marks), a response **must** include a range of points, have detailed explanation, and include accurate exemplification. Maximum of **6 marks** available (from 8 for KU) if there is no accurate or relevant exemplification.

Higher Modern Studies marking grid for 20 marks questions (KU = 8 marks; analysis/evaluation = 12 marks)

	1 mark	2 marks	3 marks	4 marks	5–6 marks
Range of relevant knowledge Accurate, relevant, up-to-date	One relevant aspect of the issue given with some description	Two relevant aspects of the issue given with some description **or** one relevant aspect covered with detailed and accurate description	One relevant aspect of the issue with detailed and accurate description **and** one relevant aspect with some description	At least two relevant aspects with detailed and accurate descriptions — these should include the key aspects of the issue	
Quality of explanation/ exemplification of knowledge Up to a maximum of **8 marks** available for knowledge and understanding	Some explanation of one aspect of the issue or relevant exemplification	Some explanation of two relevant aspects of the issue **or** detailed explanation of one aspect of the question which may include relevant exemplification	Detailed explanation of one relevant aspect of the issue with relevant exemplification **and** some explanation of one aspect of the question	At least two aspects of the question, fully explained, which relate closely to the key aspects of the question **and** extended, relevant, accurate and up-to-date exemplification	
Analysis Comments that identify relationships/implications, explore different views or establish consequences/ implications Up to **6 marks***	One relevant and accurate analytical comment	One relevant and accurate analytical comment that is justified **or** exemplified **or** two different relevant and accurate analytical comments	One developed relevant and accurate analytical comment that is justified **and** exemplified: this should relate closely to a key aspect of the question	One extended, accurate and justified analytical comment of an insightful nature which relates closely to the key aspects of the question and is exemplified	At least two developed relevant and accurate analytical comments that are justified **and** exemplified. These should relate closely to the question and may be linked for **6 marks**
Structure Structure which develops a consistent and clear line of argument Up to **2 marks**	Clear structure that addresses the issue identified in the question	Structure that clarifies the issue, presents evidence and develops a clear and consistent line of argument			
Conclusions Evaluative comments which make a judgement(s) and or reach a conclusion(s) which address the key issues in the question Up to **4 marks***	One conclusion that addresses a key issue in the question	One extended and balanced conclusion that addresses a key issue in the question **or** two conclusions that address key issues in the question	One extended and balanced conclusion that is justified and directly addresses the key issue(s) in the question **or** two balanced conclusions that address the key issues in the question, one of which is extended	One extended and balanced insightful conclusion that is justified and directly addresses the central aspects of the question **and** which considers a range of viewpoints	

*Where a candidate makes more analytical/evaluative points than are required to gain the maximum allocation of **4 marks**, these can be credited as knowledge and understanding marks provided they meet the criteria for this.

Answers to **20 marks** questions should demonstrate at least two relevant aspects of knowledge and provide detailed analysis and evaluation. For **full marks** in the KU aspect of the question (8/8), a response must include a range of points, have detailed explanation, and include a range of accurate exemplification.

Maximum of **6 marks** available (from 8 for KU) if there is no exemplification.

For **full marks** (20/20), a response must be structured, include a range of points, have detailed explanation, include a range of accurate and relevant exemplification and contain extended analysis and evaluation.

Higher Modern Studies marking grid for 8 marks source-based (objectivity/conclusions) questions

	1 mark	2 marks	3 marks	4 marks	5 marks	6 marks
Use of sources of evidence Up to **6 marks** available	One relevant piece of evidence relating to one aspect of the issue is used from one source	Two distinct pieces of evidence relating to one aspect of the issue are linked which may be from within a single source or between sources	Two distinct pieces of evidence relating to one aspect of the issue are synthesised which may be from within a single source or between sources and an evaluative commentary is given	In addition; a second aspect of the issue is addressed with reference to one relevant piece of evidence	In addition; a second aspect of the issue is addressed with reference to linked evidence	In addition; a second aspect of the issue is addressed with reference to synthesised evidence including an evaluative commentary
Objectivity Analysis of the accuracy/selectivity/objectivity of a given view against evidence is presented Up to **2 marks** available	An objective assessment of a given view is stated, based on evidence presented from the sources	A detailed objective assessment of a given view is stated, based on evidence presented from the sources	1. For **full marks** candidates **must** refer to all sources in their answer. A maximum of **6 marks** if all sources are not used. 2. **Objectivity questions.** (i) Up to **6 marks** are available for the accurate evaluation of the given view using evidence. (ii) Candidates may also be credited up to **2 marks** on any comment/analysis of the origin and reliability of the sources. (iii) Up to **2 marks** are available for an overall judgement as to the extent of accuracy/objectivity of the view. 3. **Conclusions questions.** For **full marks** candidates must make evaluative comments/judgement(s)/ draw a conclusion about each of the points given in the question. **2 further marks** are available for an overall summative conclusion.		
Conclusions Overall evaluative comment(s) derived from a judgement of the evidence presented Up to **2 marks** available	Overall conclusion is clear and supported by evidence from the sources	Overall conclusion is insightful and supported by detailed evidence from the sources				

HIGHER MODERN STUDIES
2015

Section 1 — Democracy in Scotland and the United Kingdom

Question		General Marking Instructions for this type of question	Max marks	Specific Marking Instructions for this question
1.	(a)	An analysis mark should be awarded where a candidate uses their knowledge and understanding/a source to identify relevant components (eg of an idea, theory, argument, etc) and clearly show at least one of the following: • links between different components • links between component(s) and the whole • links between component(s) and related concepts • similarities and contradictions • consistency and inconsistency • different views/interpretations • possible consequences/ implications • the relative importance of components • understanding of underlying order or structure Evaluation involves making a judgement based on criteria, drawing conclusions on the extent to which a view is supported by the evidence; the relative importance of factors; counter-arguments including possible alternative interpretations; the overall impact/ significance of the factors when taken together; the relative importance of factors in relation to the context. Credit responses that: • make reference to the political system in Scotland, the political system in the UK or the political system in Scotland and the UK • provide balanced evaluative comments referring to different factors and their relative importance/impact • provide a clear, coherent line of argument Up to **8 marks** for KU (description, explanation and exemplification) and up to **12 marks** for analytical/ evaluative comments (4 of these marks specifically for conclusions). Award up to **6 marks** per point. Where a candidate makes more analytical/evaluative points than are required to gain the maximum allocation of 8 marks, these can be credited as knowledge and understanding marks provided they meet the criteria for this.	20	***To what extent are some factors more important than others in influencing voting behaviour?*** *Candidates can be credited in a number of ways up to a maximum of 20 marks.* **Credit reference to aspects of the following:** • The different factors that influence voting behaviour • Implications of different factors influencing voting behaviour Answers may refer to: A range of factors that are said to affect voting behaviour including: • Media • Social Class • Age • Gender • Geographical location/Residence • Ethnicity • Party leader competence and Image • Issues Credit those candidates who integrate factors and highlight links between some factors, eg public perception of issues, party leader image and public awareness of party policy can be seen to be linked to media representation of these issues. Also, link between social class and occupation, education, income, etc. • Discussion of relative importance of different factors • De-alignment, long term/short term factors • Other relevant points *Any other valid point that meets the criteria described in the general marking instructions for this kind of question.* **Possible approaches to answering this questions:** **Response 1** • One factor that can affect how someone votes is the media. The media includes newspapers, television and radio as well as 'new media' such as social networking. The media plays an important role in how a leader or a political party and their policies are portrayed and parties such as the Labour Party, the Conservatives and the SNP clearly believe that the media plays a part in influencing how people vote as they spend a lot of money on spin doctors, media monitoring units and rapid rebuttal teams to ensure that the public are aware of their policies. This shows that the media can be a factor in influencing voting behaviour **(2 marks KU, 1 mark analysis).** **Response 2** • The media is also important in informing and shaping public opinion about current issues affecting the nation. Issues that have affected how people voted in recent elections include immigration, the war in Iraq and the handling of the economy. For many voters, the state of the economy is a big factor in how they vote. If the economy is doing well and people are in work and can afford a decent standard of living, they are more likely to vote for the party in power. However, if the economy is doing badly, many voters are likely to blame the government and vote for other parties. For example, following the recession of 2008, many voters blamed the former Prime Minister Gordon Brown for the poor running of the economy. At the next election in 2010, the public voted to change the government. Many voters gave the poor economy as the reason for how they voted **(2 marks KU, 3 marks analysis).**

Question	General Marking Instructions for this type of question	Max marks	Specific Marking Instructions for this question
1. (a)	(continued)		**Response 3** • Social class is an important factor which will affect the way a person votes. Society is divided into different classes depending on a person's status. It is defined based on occupation, income, education and home ownership. Classes are divided into A, B, C, D and E, with those in social class A and B usually in a professional occupation such as accountants or surgeons. Those in groups D or E would include the poorest who may be in unskilled work or unemployed. Historically election results have shown that those in A and B often support the Conservatives, whilst DE voters support Labour because Labour policies such as Tax Credits and the National Minimum Wage have benefitted the poorest. However class dealignment means that there is an increase in middle classes and so the role of social class is less influential. In 2010 40% of DE voters, voted Labour. Therefore social class is an important factor, but not as important as it used to be (**5 marks KU, 2 marks analysis**).
(b)	An analysis mark should be awarded where a candidate uses their knowledge and understanding/a source to identify relevant components (eg of an idea, theory, argument, etc) and clearly show at least one of the following: • links between different components • links between component(s) and the whole • links between component(s) and related concepts • similarities and contradictions • consistency and inconsistency • different views/interpretations • possible consequences/implications • the relative importance of components • understanding of underlying order or structure Evaluation involves making a judgement based on criteria, drawing conclusions on the extent to which a view is supported by the evidence; counter-arguments including possible alternative interpretations; the overall impact/significance of the factors when taken together; the relative importance of factors in relation to the context. Credit responses that: • make reference to the political system in Scotland, the political system in the UK or the political system in Scotland and the UK • provide balanced evaluative comments referring to the effectiveness of different forms of participation and their relative importance/impact • provide a clear, coherent line of argument	20	*Most citizens participate effectively in the political process.* *Discuss* *Candidates can be credited in a number of ways up to a maximum of 20 marks.* **Credit reference to aspects of the following:** • The various methods of participation in politics • The effectiveness of different types of participation Answers may refer to: The various methods of participation in politics: • Voting • Joining a party/campaigning • Pressure group membership/participation • Protest – various forms legal or illegal • Participation through interaction with the media • Standing for election at various levels **Possible approaches to answering the question:** **Response 1** • UK citizens can participate simply by voting for representatives at various elections. An example of this would be the last UK General Election when almost 30 million citizens voted in 650 constituencies and returned a coalition government made up of MPs from the Liberal Democrats and Conservatives (**2 marks KU**). **Response 2** • Many Scottish people voted in the recent Independence referendum. The turnout for this referendum was almost 85%, an extremely high participation rate. Many scots believed it was their responsibility to participate in this way as the issue in question was so important. The high turnout added legitimacy to the eventual "No" result and shows that registering and participating was effective. This was the first time many Scots had actually registered to vote. Many argue that this increased participation has actually changed Scotland for good, making it a more democratic country (**1 mark KU – 1 mark analysis, 1 mark evaluation**).

Question		General Marking Instructions for this type of question	Max marks	Specific Marking Instructions for this question
1.	(b)	(continued) Up to **8 marks** for KU (description, explanation and exemplification) and up to **12 marks** for analytical/evaluative comments. Award up to **6 marks** per point. Where a candidate makes more analytical/evaluative points than are required to gain the maximum allocation of **4 marks**, these can be credited as knowledge and understanding marks provided they meet the criteria for this.		**Response 3** • Many citizens take part in pressure group activity in the UK. Some groups (insider groups such as the CBI) are effective in their activities and have close links to government. However, some "outsider groups" are less successful in their campaigns as they are seen as being hostile to government and are often demanding radical changes. A group such as Greenpeace has many thousands of members who are participating in the political process through their membership but their activities are often unsuccessful in changing government environmental policy. Groups like this have often taken part in activities which may be illegal thus reducing their effectiveness in winning over public and government opinion. Many citizens do participate in the political process, but not all are effective **(3 marks KU, 2 marks analysis, 1 mark evaluation).** **Response 4** • Most UK citizens do not participate in any effective way in the political process. Many never vote in any election. Turnouts at local council elections and European elections often fall below 30%. Many others do vote but due to the electoral system, especially in Westminster elections, their votes are ineffective as they support a candidate from a minor party such as the Greens who have little chance of winning their constituency or forming the government. Participation is seen as ineffective by these people as they feel unable to influence the result **(2 marks KU, 2 marks evaluation).** *Any other valid point that meets the criteria described in the general marking principles for this kind of question.*

Section 2 – Social Issues in the United Kingdom

Question	General Marking Instructions for this type of question	Max marks	Specific Marking Instructions for this question
2.	The candidate is required to interpret/evaluate up to three complex sources of information detecting and explaining the extent of objectivity. In order to achieve credit candidates must show evidence which supports the extent of accuracy in a given viewpoint. • Award up to 3 marks for appropriate use of evidence depending on the quality of the explanation and the synthesis of the evidence for any one explanation of the extent of objectivity. • For **full marks** candidates must refer to all sources in their answer. • For **full marks** candidates must make an overall judgment as to the extent of the accuracy of the given statement. • Maximum of 6 marks if no overall judgement made on extent of accuracy of the statement. • Candidates may be awarded up to a maximum of 2 marks for incorporating an evaluation of the reliability of the sources in their explanations although this is not mandatory.	8	*To what extent is it accurate to state that the government's anti-smoking policies are successfully tackling the problem of smoking in Scotland?* *Candidates can be credited in a number of ways up to a maximum of 8 marks.* **Evidence that supports the view ("the government's anti-smoking policies are successfully tackling the problem of smoking in Scotland?")** **Examples of the types of evidence that support the view include:** • Source A, 23% of adults smoke in Scotland, less than a quarter and a downward trend backed by Source B: 23% of all adults smoke. • Source C, smoking rates for all young people who are regular smokers are declining both boys and girls and predicted to remain steady. • Source C, 13yr old girls and boys are now virtually the same or lower than before. • Source C, 3 of the 4 groups shown have all declined since 2006 (all but 15yr old boys) link to smoking ban in Source A. • Source A: Only 10% of people living in the least deprived areas smoke. Link to Source B: levels below the average of 23% include those in full time employment 22% and those who are self-employed 22%. • Source A: Less than one quarter (23%) of adults smoked in 2013 which continues a general downwards trend in the proportion of adults who smoke. Link to Source C: this trend continues in young people as the number has decreased or remained steady.

Question	General Marking Instructions for this type of question	Max marks	Specific Marking Instructions for this question
2.	(continued)		• Source C, rates for young smokers have reduced dramatically since 1996 (30%) to around 15% in 2012, so the message is getting through.

Response 1

The number of adults smoking is falling according to Source 1. This is backed by the downward trend in 13 and 15 year olds smoking as shown in Source C. This shows that since 2006 smoking has fallen amongst all groups, most especially among 15 year old girls. This figure has fallen by 5% since 2006. The smoking ban and increasing the age to buy cigarettes to 18 may have helped cause this, a clear success of policy **(3 marks, evidence synthesised from two sources with evaluative comment).**

Evidence that opposes the view ("the government's anti-smoking policies are successfully tackling the problem of smoking in Scotland?")

• Source A: Smoking is the main cause of early death.
• Source A, cost to NHS remains high, £271m/yr.
• Source A: 13,000 deaths per year where smoking is the main cause of death.
• Source A: As many as 600 children take up smoking each day. Scotland has the highest rate behind England.
• Source A: 39% of those in the most deprived areas in Scotland smoke, Link to Source B: deprived areas tend to high level so unemployment, 51% of adult unemployed and looking for work smoke, supported by link to Source A which states those out of work are most likely to smoke.
• Source B: highest rate of adult smokers 60%, those who are unable to work due to short term illness, sick or disabled (51%) also links to Source A which states those out of work are most likely to smoke.
• Source A: despite all previous attempts to reduce smoking among young people, age increased to 18yrs, restrictions on cigarette displays, 50 children a day start smoking in Scotland.
• Source C, 15yr old girls continue to become regular smokers, 12%, this is higher than boys. Link to Source A: previous attempts to target smoking in young people.
• Source A: Scottish Government continues to target smoking in its policy, trying to stop young people starting.
• Scotland has the highest smoking rates in the UK, 23%.

Response 2

The policies of the government are not successful in tackling smoking in Scotland as 23% of Scots still smoke which is the highest **(1 mark, one relevant piece of evidence from one source).**

Candidates may also be credited up **to** 2 marks on any comment/analysis of the origin and reliability of the source.
• Information from Source B is taken from the Scottish Government's website which has a responsibility to publish accurate and recent data for public information **(1 mark).**
• Information from Source C is taken from ASH Scotland, is a well-known voluntary organisation that provides evidence based information on tobacco. However it may be seen as biased as it receives some of its funding from Scottish Government which is committed to cutting smoking rates **(2 marks).**

Question	General Marking Instructions for this type of question	Max marks	Specific Marking Instructions for this question
2.	(continued)		• The information in Source A is adapted from a BBC news article published online with additional information from Cancer Research UK. As the article has been adapted it may be less reliable than when originally written. Also it is not clear what parts come from exactly which source **(2 marks)**.
			• Statistics in Source A are up to date (2012, 2013) **(0 marks)**.
			• Statistics in Source A are up to date (2012, 2013) and so give a fairly up to date picture of the smoking issue **(1 mark)**.
			For **full marks**, candidates **must** make an overall judgment as to the extent of the accuracy of the given statement.
			Overall, the evidence **does** support the view as:
			• On the whole, the evidence suggests that smoking is being successfully tackled by the government's policies. The number of adults smoking is falling. It may still be higher in Scotland than in any other country in the UK but importantly the number of young smokers is falling rapidly as shown in Source C this is also backed by the extremely low number of schoolchildren smoking, only 3% **(2 marks)**.
			• The statement is mostly true as smoking is a declining problem as can be seen from Source C. There are still too many children starting to smoke so the government's policies may be slow, but they are working **(1 mark)**.
			The statement is partly true as fewer adults are smoking (23% and falling) possibly as a result of the smoking ban which was introduced in 2006. However, those who are unemployed or dependent on benefits have not been helped as is shown in Source B, over half of those in the three categories, Unemployed, Disabled and short term illness are smokers **(2 marks)**.

Part A: Social inequality in the UK

Question		General Marking Instructions for this type of question	Max marks	Specific Marking Instructions for this question
3.	(a)	Evaluation involves making a judgement(s) based on criteria, drawing conclusions on the extent to which a view is supported by the evidence; counter-arguments including possible alternative interpretations; the overall impact/significance of the factors when taken together; the relative importance of factors in relation to the context. Up to **8 marks** for KU (description, explanation and exemplification) and up to **4 marks** for evaluative comments. Award up to **6 marks** per point. Candidates should be credited up to **full marks** if they answer within a Scottish context only, a UK context only or refer to both Scotland and the UK. Where a candidate makes more evaluative points than are required to gain the maximum allocation of **4 marks**, these can be credited as knowledge and understanding marks provided they meet the criteria for this.	12	*Evaluate the view that social inequality affects some groups in society more than others* *Candidates can be credited in a number of ways up to a maximum of 12 marks.* Credit responses that make reference to: • the nature of social inequality • socio-economic groups and the impact of inequalities on them • an evaluation of the importance of various socio-economic factors in causing inequality Credit reference to aspects of the following: • Age groups • Ethnicity • Gender • Class • Disability • Health Inequalities • Income Inequalities • Housing Inequalities • Education • Crime • Discrimination • Family structure • Poverty *Any other valid point that meets the criteria described in the general marking principles for this kind of question.* **Possible approaches to answering the question:** **Response 1** • Groups who do not do well in the education system may not find a job and so will be unemployed and have to rely on benefits **(1 mark KU)**. **Response 2** • Women in the UK are more likely to be living in poverty. One reason may be that they are more likely to be the head of a single parent family. This creates obvious pressures on time and often results in welfare dependency for the family. Recent statistics show that around 90% of lone parent families are headed by a woman and over 25% of children now live with a lone mother **(2 marks KU)**. **Response 3** • There are major inequalities in health affecting certain groups in the UK. Life expectancy among the poorest people in Scotland is much lower than among the richest. Within Glasgow, male life expectancy varies by as much as twenty seven years between the poorest and richest areas. Poor health certainly affects the poorest more as a result of lifestyle choices which are limited partly by low income. Poor diet and a lack of exercise are the main causes of health problems for our poorest groups. Many Scots choose to eat too much fatty food and healthy eating campaigns, such as the 5-a-day campaign, have had less impact on poorer areas where fresh fruit and vegetables are not only less easily available but are often too expensive. Such issues do not affect those on higher incomes who can afford fresh food and can travel more easily to a wider variety of shops. The poorest groups in society suffer greater ill health which leads to lower earnings, lower educational attainment etc ie multiple deprivation. As a result the poor will continue to suffer health inequalities **(3 marks KU, 2 marks evaluation)**.

Question		General Marking Instructions for this type of question	Max marks	Specific Marking Instructions for this question
3.	(a)	(continued)		**Response 4** • Some people would question the link between poverty and social inequality. They would claim that many people have become successful even although they came from a poor community with few amenities and were not encouraged to succeed in education. For example, Brian Souter has become very wealthy through starting several transport companies. He is the son of a bus driver and certainly not from a wealthy background. However, although there may be cases of successful people from poor backgrounds evidence shows that people from wealthy middle class families are more likely to go to university and therefore more likely to have much higher lifetime earnings. Consequently, poor children are likely to grow up poor adults **(1 mark KU, 3 marks evaluation)**. *Any other valid point that meets the criteria described in the general marking principles for this kind of question.*
	(b)	Evaluation involves making a judgement(s) based on criteria, drawing conclusions on the extent to which a view is supported by the evidence; counter-arguments including possible alternative interpretations; the overall impact/significance of the factors when taken together; the relative importance of factors in relation to the context. Up to **8 marks** for KU (description, explanation and exemplification) and up to **4 marks** for evaluative comments. Award up to **6 marks** per point. Candidates should be credited up to **full marks** if they answer within a Scottish context only, a UK context only or refer to both Scotland and the UK. Where a candidate makes more evaluative point than are required to gain the maximum allocation of **4 marks**, these can be credited as knowledge and understanding marks provided they meet the criteria for this.	12	*Evaluate the effectiveness of <u>either</u> the benefits system <u>or</u> health services in tackling social inequality.* Credit responses that make reference to: • the role of the benefits system in tackling inequality • an evaluation of the success/shortcomings of the benefits system in tackling social inequality OR Credit responses that make reference to: • the role of health services (public and/or private) in tackling inequality • an evaluation of the success/shortcomings of health services in tackling social inequality *Candidates can be credited in a number of ways **up to a maximum of 12 marks.*** Possible approaches to answering the question: **Response 1** • UK citizens who have no other source of income or are on a low income are helped by a wide range of welfare benefits provided by central government. The old age pension, universal benefit and housing benefit are just three which try to meet the needs of many people **(2 marks KU)**. **Response 2** • Child benefit is paid to families who earn below a certain amount to help with the additional costs of bringing up children. The amount paid is £20.50 per week for the eldest child and £13.55 for each additional child. This helps to tackle inequality as these payments are very important to those who have a very low income and make a big difference to the family income in a poor household. Child benefit is not paid in full to households with a high income — after £50,000 the amount of child benefit paid is reduced. This means that it helps to reduce inequality as families on low income get more in benefit than high-income families **(2 marks KU, 1 mark evaluation)**.

Question	General Marking Instructions for this type of question	Max marks	Specific Marking Instructions for this question
3. (b)	(continued)		**Response 3** • Critics would claim that the National Health Service is not effective in tackling inequality as it is under-staffed and under-funded. Recent media coverage has concentrated on the winter pressures faced by Accident and Emergency departments across the UK. Many of the departments have failed to meet targets set for them regarding waiting and discharge times. However, it could also be argued that as a society we expect so much from the NHS that it is almost certain to fail to meet these expectations. Despite its problems and failings the NHS has contributed hugely to tackling social inequality in the UK. Without its universal, free at the point of need principles then the majority of citizens would struggle to afford healthcare. Life expectancy and infant mortality figures have improved greatly for the poorest since the NHS was introduced. If we are to maintain these improvements then we will either have to reorganise the NHS, lower our expectations or be willing to pay more tax to fund it. Overall, the NHS has been vital in improving the living conditions in our society **(2 marks KU, 3 marks evaluation)**. **Response 4** • Many in the UK now rely on private health care as well as the government funded NHS. Over 15% of all that is spent on health care in the UK is spent by the private sector rather than by the NHS. This creates a divide in society and effectively makes inequality worse. Those who can afford to go private can skip the queue and those who can't have to wait for a poorer service from the NHS **(1 mark KU, 2 marks evaluation)**. *Any other valid point that meets the criteria described in the general marking principles for this kind of question.*

Part B: Crime and the law in the UK

Question	General Marking Instructions for this type of question	Max marks	Specific Marking Instructions for this question
3. (c)	Evaluation involves making a judgement(s) based on criteria, drawing conclusions on the extent to which a view is supported by the evidence; counter-arguments including possible alternative interpretations; the overall impact/significance of the factors when taken together; the relative importance of factors in relation to the context. Up to **8 marks** for KU (description, explanation and exemplification) and up to **4 marks** for evaluative comments. Award up to **6 marks** per point. Candidates should be credited up to **full marks** if they answer within a Scottish context only, a UK context only or refer to both Scotland and the UK.	12	*Evaluate the view that crime only affects the victims.* Credit responses that make reference to: • the personal impact of crime on the individual • an evaluation of the relative impact of crime on family, community, wider society, economy, government etc Credit reference to aspects of the following: • likely victims — age, gender, race etc • physical impact • psychological impact • economic/financial impact • impact on families • impact on local community • impact on local business • impact on wider society • impact on offender • political/legal impact — eg new anti-terror legislation *Any other valid point that meets the criteria described in the general marking principles for this kind of question.* *Candidates can be credited in a number of ways up to a maximum of 12 marks.*

Question		General Marking Instructions for this type of question	Max marks	Specific Marking Instructions for this question
3.	(c)	(continued) Where a candidate makes more evaluative point than are required to gain the maximum allocation of 4 marks, these can be credited as knowledge and understanding marks provided they meet the criteria for this.		**Possible approaches to answering the question:** **Response 1** • Assaulting a person is a crime. The person may need to go to hospital as they have been injured. As well as a physical injury the crime may leave a psychological injury on the victim ie they may be scared to go out and have no confidence. The victim is affected in two ways **(1 mark KU, 1 mark evaluation)**. **Response 2** • It is not just the direct victim of a crime who is affected by it. There could also be an impact on their family. If the person is severely injured then they may be unable to return to work meaning a drop in income and all the difficulties this may bring eg poorer lifestyle, diet, health etc. In this way crime can affect a much wider group. The family of the offender may also be affected by the crime. They may feel ashamed and be shunned by their community. These are often more serious and longer lasting than the initial physical damage to the victim. It is too simplistic to say that only the "victim" is affected **(3 marks evaluation)**. **Response 3** • Often the whole community is affected by a criminal act. From the actions of only a very small group of offenders a local area can gain a "bad" reputation if there is too much violent crime. For example, some parts of Glasgow have a reputation for violent gang crime. This can have a negative effect on the spirit of the people who live there but can also have a negative effect on the area's economy. If people don't want to live there then house prices may drop. Household and car insurance in the area may become more expensive, further driving people away. People who stay will have less to spend. Local business may not wish to be associated with the area leading them to relocate. Unemployment may then rise further reducing the desirability of the area. Local business will of course suffer as they may have to pay higher insurance premiums etc. Overall, to suggest that crime only affects the victim is clearly wrong. It can have a negative impact on the social and economic life of an entire community. On the other hand the impact of a major crime could bring a community together and create a determination among people that the community will get over it and grow stronger. A good example of this was the midnight anti-rape protests which took place in Glasgow in order to support the victims and to show solidarity against criminals **(3 marks KU, 3 marks evaluation)**. *Any other valid point that meets the criteria described in the general marking principles for this kind of question.*

Question		General Marking Instructions for this type of question	Max marks	Specific Marking Instructions for this question
3.	(d)	Evaluation involves making a judgement(s) based on criteria, drawing conclusions on the extent to which a view is supported by the evidence; counter-arguments including possible alternative interpretations; the overall impact/significance of the factors when taken together; the relative importance of factors in relation to the context. Up to **8 marks** for KU (description, explanation and exemplification) and up to **4 marks** for evaluative comments. Award up to **6 marks** per point. Candidates should be credited up to **full marks** if they answer within a Scottish context only, a UK context only or refer to both Scotland and the UK. Where a candidate makes more evaluative points than are required to gain the maximum allocation of **4 marks**, these can be credited as knowledge and understanding marks provided they meet the criteria for this.	12	*Evaluate the effectiveness of either prison sentences or community based sentences in tackling crime.* Credit responses that make reference to: • the role of prison sentences in tackling crime • an evaluation of the success/shortcomings of prison sentences in tackling crime Credit responses that make reference to: • the role of community based sentences in tackling crime • an evaluation of the success/shortcomings of community based sentences in tackling crime *Candidates can be credited in a number of ways up to a maximum of 12 marks.* **Possible approaches to answering the question:** **Response 1** • Prison is an effective way of tackling crime because someone who is locked up in prison is not free to be on the street and attack people (**1 mark KU**). **Response 2** • Prison is not an effective way of tackling crime as prisons are often overcrowded and short-staffed. This means that prisoners are often locked up for most of the day and prisons are unable to carry out much rehabilitation — such as education classes to give prisoners skills to help them get a job when they are released from prison. As a result, there is a high rate of recidivism with people who are released from prison going on to commit more crimes and being returned to prison for another sentence (**2 marks KU, 1 mark evaluation**). **Response 3** • Prison can be an effective method of tackling crime as it involves the loss of freedom and so is a form of punishment. This will act as a deterrent to many people and stop them from committing a crime as they would fear being locked up for a period of time away from their friends and families (**2 marks evaluation**). **Response 4** • Community based sentences are very effective in tackling crime as they allow offenders to maintain daily contact with their family and loved ones. This means they do not feel isolated and do not grow anxious about the events affecting their family while they are in prison. If an offender is placed on a Community Order they will be ordered to carry out a certain number of hours of work which they can do in their spare time, allowing them to keep their job. This is an obvious advantage in stopping recidivism. Part of the order may also see them being given help for any addiction issues they may have. This sense of value that is created in the offender will make them much less likely to re-offend and the financial cost to the community will be low eg average cost of a Community Payback Order is only £2400 (**2 marks KU, 2 marks evaluation**). **Response 5** • The majority of the public think community based sentences are no more than a slap on the wrists for criminals. It is clear they have little impact on crime by the fact that around 30% on CPOs breach the orders and use the opportunity to further offend (**1 mark KU, 1 mark evaluation**). *Any other valid point that meets the criteria described in the general marking principles for this kind of question.*

Question	General Marking Instructions for this type of question	Max marks	Specific Marking Instructions for this question
4.	The candidate is required to interpret/evaluate up to three complex sources in order to reach conclusions. In order to achieve credit candidates must show evidence which explains the conclusions reached. Award up to **3 marks** for appropriate use of evidence depending on the quality of the explanation and the synthesis of the evidence to reach any one conclusion. For **full marks** candidates must refer to all sources in their answer. For **full marks** candidates must reach conclusions about each of the points given and make an overall conclusion on the issue.	8	*What conclusions can be drawn about the impact of the recession on different EU members?* *Candidates can be credited in a number of ways up to a maximum of 8 marks.* **Possible approaches to answering the question:** **The economic impact of the recession on Eurozone members** **Response 1** • Source A states that, the recession led to some serious long term economic problems for Eurozone countries. This is supported by Source B which shows that the biggest increase in unemployment was in Cyprus, where it quadrupled. This shows that the recession has had a huge impact on the Eurozone countries **(2 marks, synthesis of evidence across Sources A and B with conclusion)**. **Response 2** • The recession clearly had a negative effect on all Eurozone countries but not all to the same extent. This is shown by the example of Spain from Source B which has a debt of 72% of its GDP which is lower than the EU average of 89% and by the example of Ireland which was more seriously affected as its debt has increased to 123% of GDP, which is much higher than the EU figure and is nearly five times higher than it was **(3 marks for complex synthesis between Sources A and B and a conclusion)**. **The economic impact of the recession on Non-Eurozone members** **Response 3** • The recession had smaller effect on Non-Eurozone countries. As Source C shows Denmark has seen its unemployment rate rise to 7% but this is 3% less than the EU average **(2 marks, detailed synthesis across Sources A and C)**. **Response 4** • The recession has not had such a serious effect on Non-Eurozone members. Several Eurozone countries have required "hand-outs" from the EU to help them cope with their huge debts eg both Ireland and Spain needed a 90billion Euro hand-out. This hasn't been needed for any non-Eurozone countries who all, apart from the UK, have a level of debt below the EU figure (89% of GDP). In fact, one non Eurozone country, Sweden, did not increase its levels of debt at all as a result of the recession. All of the Non-Eurozone countries in Source C have unemployment rates below the EU average **(3 marks synthesis and detailed use of sources)**. **Possible overall conclusion about the impact of the recession on the EU as a whole** **Response 5** • The overall conclusion is that the EU as a whole has suffered badly from the recession but the Eurozone members suffered the most. Source A shows that the level of exports to countries outside the EU has dropped by 4% which may have resulted in the large increases in unemployment and debt levels in countries like Portugal **(2 marks for a valid overall conclusion based on evidence)**. **Response 6** • The overall conclusion is that the recession has not had an equal impact across the EU's members. Some have suffered very badly from higher unemployment and debt eg Spain unemployment doubled and they need a bail out to survive whereas the UK had only a small increase in unemployment and Sweden did not increase its borrowing at all **(2 marks for a valid overall conclusion based on evidence)**. **Please note that a valid conclusion which is not supported with relevant source evidence should be given no credit.** *Any other valid point that meets the criteria described in the general marking principles for this kind of question.*

Section 3 — International Issues

Question		General Marking Instructions for this type of question	Max marks	Specific Marking Instructions for this question
5.	(a)	An analysis mark should be awarded where a candidate uses their knowledge and understanding/a source to identify relevant components (eg of an idea, theory, argument, etc) and clearly show at least one of the following: • links between different components • links between component(s) and the whole • links between component(s) and related concepts • similarities and contradictions • consistency and inconsistency • different views/interpretations • possible consequences/implications • the relative importance of components • understanding of underlying order or structure Up to **8 marks** for KU (description, explanation and exemplification) and up to **4 marks** for analytical comments. Award up to **6 marks** per point. Where a candidate makes more analytical points than are required to gain the maximum allocation of **4 marks**, these can be credited as knowledge and understanding marks provided they meet the criteria for this.	12	*With reference to a world power you have studied, analyse the ability of this world power to influence other countries.* Credit responses that make reference to: • the world power's unilateral influence on its neighbours • the importance of the world power in wider international relations eg through organisations such as the UN or NATO • overall evaluative comment on the importance of the world power in influencing other countries • provide a clear, coherent line of argument **Possible approaches to answering the question:** **World Power: USA** **Credit reference to aspects of the following:** • member of the UN Security Council • examples of US involvement in Afghanistan (ISAF) • leading role in NATO — examples of US involvement in Libya as part of Operation Unified Protector • possible future role of US in Syria • mèmber of the G8 • largest economy in the world • role in Middle East • nuclear superpower • impact of emergence of China as superpower • economic, social and cultural impact on immediate neighbours such as Mexico and Canada and on North/central America as a whole including Cuba *Any other valid point that meets the criteria described in the general marking principles for this kind of question.* **World Power: China** **Credit reference to aspects of the following:** • leading role as a permanent member of the UN Security Council • participates in UN peace-keeping operations • relationship with and future role in negotiations with North Korea • impact of US/China diplomatic relations • investment in African countries and elsewhere • growing importance of China in world economy (2nd to the USA and expected to pass) • member of the G20 • part of the G8's Outreach Five (O5) • economic, social and cultural impact on immediate neighbours such as India and North Korea and on Asia as a whole *Any other valid point that meets the criteria described in the general marking principles for this kind of question.* **Possible approaches to answering the question:** **World Power: USA** **Response 1** • The USA's role as a world power is very important. It was one of the original countries that set up NATO in 1949 and still remains its most influential member. More recently the USA has played the lead role in NATO's mission to Afghanistan (ISAF) **(2 marks KU).**

Question		General Marking Instructions for this type of question	Max marks	Specific Marking Instructions for this question
5.	(a)	(continued)		**Response 2** • The USA's role as a world power is very important. It was one of the original countries that set up NATO in 1949 and still remains its most influential member. More recently the USA has played the lead role in NATO's mission to Afghanistan (ISAF). In terms of finance, troop and resource commitments to NATO, the USA provides far more than any other single member of the Alliance making the US the most important member of NATO with huge influence **(2 marks KU, 1 mark analysis).** **Response 3** • The USA's role as a world power is very important. It was one of the original countries that set up NATO in 1949 and remains its most influential member. More recently the USA has played the lead role in NATO's mission to Afghanistan (ISAF). In terms of finance, troop and resource commitments to NATO, the USA provides far more than any other single member of the Alliance making the US the most important member of NATO with huge influence. However, in recent years the USA has called on the other members of NATO to pay a greater share of the organisation's costs. The USA has also reduced its commitments in Europe, expecting the European members of NATO to take over. Although the USA can dominate NATO in terms of its contribution, all NATO's 28 member states have equal standing, ie no one member country has more voting rights than the next and there must be agreement by all before action can be taken. The USA has huge influence, but NATO is not always obliged to follow its lead as the other members can out vote them. However, this does not always stop the USA which has the capacity to act alone **(2 marks KU, 4 marks analysis).** **Response 4** • Therefore, given the importance of the USA within NATO, the UN, other international bodies and the global economy, it is clear the USA is, at present, the world's most influential country. For example, the US is sometimes described as 'the leader of the free world'. However, countries such as China and India are closing the gap in terms of economic output and world influence. Further, China has entered the space race and is increasing its influence in Africa. Also, despite US/NATO military strength in Afghanistan, they have failed to completely defeat the Taliban. The USA may be the worlds' only 'superpower' but this does not mean it can control everything **(4 marks analysis).**

Question		General Marking Instructions for this type of question	Max marks	Specific Marking Instructions for this question

5.	(b)	An analysis mark should be awarded where a candidate uses their knowledge and understanding/a source to identify relevant components (eg of an idea, theory, argument, etc) and clearly show at least one of the following:
		• links between different components
		• links between component(s) and the whole
		• links between component(s) and related concepts
		• similarities and contradictions
		• consistency and inconsistency
		• different views/interpretations
		• possible consequences/implications
		• the relative importance of components
		• understanding of underlying order or structure
		
		Up to **8 marks** for KU (description, explanation and exemplification) and up to **4 marks** for analytical comments.
		
		Award up to **6 marks** per point.
		
		Where a candidate makes more analytical points than are required to gain the maximum allocation of **4 marks**, these can be credited as knowledge and understanding marks provided they meet the criteria for this.
			12	*With reference to a world power you have studied, analyse the impact of a recent social issue on this world power.*
				
				Credit references that make reference to:
				• Description/explanation of the social issue
				• Impact of the social issue on specific groups or the country as a whole
				
				Candidates can be credited in a number of ways up to a maximum of 12 marks.
				
				Credit reference to aspects of the following:
				
				• Impact of issues concerning:
				  • Healthcare
				  • Education
				  • Housing
				  • Crime
				  • Population/Immigration
				  • Economy — welfare/poverty
				  • Environmental
				
				World Power Choice: India
				
				Response 1
				• The population of India has continued to grow in recent years. They now have 17% of the world's population (1.21 billion people). India is expected to have more people than China by the year 2030, creating huge problems for housing, healthcare etc **(2 marks KU)**.
				
				Response 2
				• The population of India has continued to grow in recent years. They now have 17% of the world's population (1.21 billion people). India is expected to have more people than China by the year 2030, creating huge problems for housing, healthcare etc. The population has grown by 181 million in the last ten years putting massive pressure on already stretched educational services. On top of an extremely high birth rate life expectancy has grown by ten years to an average of 75. The demand for healthcare created by an ageing population is financially difficult for the government **(2 marks KU, 2 marks analysis)**.
				
				Response 3
				• The population of India has continued to grow in recent years. They now have 17% of the world's population (1.21 billion people). India is expected to have more people than China by the year 2030, creating huge problems for housing, healthcare etc. The population has grown by 181 million in the last ten years putting massive pressure on already stretched educational services. On top of an extremely high birth rate life expectancy has grown by ten years to an average of 75. The demand for healthcare created by an ageing population is financially difficult for the government. The ageing of the population is perhaps the most serious social problem facing India. Over 100 million people are elderly and although over 60% of the population is under thirty the cost of healthcare and pensions for the elderly is enormous. The average Indian worker does not earn enough to pay large amounts of tax **(3 marks KU, 3 marks analysis)**.
				
				Also credit reference to aspects of1 the following:
				• Growing economy
				• Widening gap between urban and rural areas
				• Women's rights and progress

Question		General Marking Instructions for this type of question	Max marks	Specific Marking Instructions for this question
5.	**(b)**	(continued)		**World Power choice: China**

Response 4
- Rapid growth in the Chinese population has been a problem for many decades. Since the 1970s the Chinese Government has enforced measures to control the number of children people can have. Couples can have only one child in urban areas but can have two in rural areas, provided the first-born is a girl. This was known as the One Child Policy **(2 marks KU)**.

Response 5
- Rapid growth in the Chinese population has been a problem for many decades. Since the 1970s the Chinese Government has enforced measures to control the number of children people can have. Couples can have only one child in urban areas but can have two in rural areas, provided the first-born is a girl. This was known as the One Child Policy. Punishments for couples who had too many children ranged from fines, loss of employment to forced abortions and sterilizations during the later stages of their pregnancy **(3 marks KU)**.

Response 6
- Rapid growth in the Chinese population has been a problem for many decades. Since the 1970s the Chinese Government has enforced measures to control the number of children people can have. Couples can have only one child in urban areas but can have two in rural areas, provided the first-born is a girl. This was known as the One Child Policy. Punishments for couple who had too many children ranged from fines, loss of employment to forced abortions and sterilizations during the later stages of their pregnancy. The policy was strictly enforced throughout the final decades of the twentieth century and as a result there has been an increase in the number of children forced to carry the burden of caring for ageing parents on their own.

Fewer girls than boys survived to adulthood as many people, especially in rural areas, abandoned or killed their first born baby if it was a girl. In many traditional areas boys became even more valuable than girls.

This created a gender imbalance affecting the population and the economy. However there is evidence that the One Child Policy will be relaxed in some areas. Families will be allowed two children if one parent is an only child and fines have been lowered **(4 marks KU, 3 marks analysis)**.

Also credit reference to aspects of the following:
- Widening gap between rural and urban areas
- Impact of growing economy and investment in market economy
- Media censorship

Question		General Marking Instructions for this type of question	Max marks	Specific Marking Instructions for this question
5.	(c)	An analysis mark should be awarded where a candidate uses their knowledge and understanding/a source to identify relevant components (eg of an idea, theory, argument, etc) and clearly show at least one of the following: • links between different components • links between component(s) and the whole • links between component(s) and related concepts • similarities and contradictions • consistency and inconsistency • different views/interpretations • possible consequences/implications • the relative importance of components • understanding of underlying order or structure Up to **8 marks** for KU (description, explanation and exemplification) and up to **4 marks** for analytical comments Award up to **6 marks** per point. Where a candidate makes more analytical points than are required to gain the maximum allocation of **4 marks**, these can be credited as knowledge and understanding marks provided they meet the criteria for this.	12	*With reference to a world issue you have studied, analyse the role of international organisations in attempting to resolve this issue* *Candidates can be credited in a number of ways up to a maximum of 12 marks.* Depending on the world issue chosen, candidates may analyse aspects such as: • The nature of issue • The international organisations involved • The nature of responses to the organisation's actions • Success and failure of the organisation's actions and the reasons for these successes and failures **Poverty in Africa:** **Response 1** • Poverty in Africa is often caused by ill-health. One of the most serious diseases in Africa is Malaria which affects millions of Africans, killing hundreds of thousands every year. People who are ill cannot work and so they and their families fall deeper into poverty. The World Health Organisation (WHO), which is part of the United Nations, is responsible for improving health around the world. The WHO has attempted to tackle malaria by providing drugs to treat people in poor areas. They have also provided millions of nets sprayed with insecticide to protect people when they are sleeping or praying. This is an effective way of controlling the mosquitoes which spread the disease and has resulted in many saved lives. However, their response to malaria is still considered inadequate by many as each of these nets only costs a few pounds yet one African child dies every sixty seconds as a result of malaria (**3 marks KU, 2 marks analysis**). **Response 2** • During recent civil wars many people have become refugees as their homes have been destroyed by armed men. They now live in poverty as a result (**1 mark KU**). **Response 3** • Many children in countries like Botswana have been left orphaned by AIDS. This has denied them an education and resulted in a lifetime of poverty. Their health will also be affected as what little healthcare that may be available, they will be unable to afford (**2 marks KU**). **Syria:** • condemnation of Syrian government by UN, Arab League, western countries • sanctions, including economic sanctions • UN investigation/inspection of use of chemical weapons • humanitarian assistance for refugees • aid to anti-government forces • threats of military action/intervention **Terrorism:** • Growth of IS, Boko Haram, Al-Shabaab etc • "home-grown" terrorists — Paris attacks etc • Religious/ethnic/political conflicts • NATO — Article 5 (Collective defence), vast resources committed by NATO, Operation Active Endeavour, help in providing security at major events such as Olympic games and European Football championships etc.

Question		General Marking Instructions for this type of question	Max marks	Specific Marking Instructions for this question
5.	(c)	(continued)		• The UN — coordinating action through the Security Council and the General Assembly, The United Nations Global Counter-Terrorism Strategy • The African Union Counter Terrorism framework • The European Union Counter terrorism Strategy — focusing on stopping the causes of radicalisation and recruitment etc, tries to improve the sharing of information between member states, European arrest warrant strengthened etc *Any other valid point that meets the criteria described in the general marking principles for this kind of question.*

	(d)	An analysis mark should be awarded where a candidate uses their knowledge and understanding/a source to identify relevant components (eg of an idea, theory, argument, etc) and clearly show at least one of the following:
		• links between different components
		• links between component(s) and the whole
		• links between component(s) and related concepts
		• similarities and contradictions
		• consistency and inconsistency
		• different views/interpretations
		• possible consequences/implications
		• the relative importance of components
		• understanding of underlying order or structure
		
		Up to **8 marks** for KU (description, explanation and exemplification) and up to **4 marks** for analytical comments.
		
		Award up to **6 marks** per point.
		
		Where a candidate makes more analytical points than are required to gain the maximum allocation of **4 marks**, these can be credited as knowledge and understanding marks provided they meet the criteria for this.
			12	*With reference to a world issue you have studied; analyse the different factors which have caused this issue.*
				
				*Candidates can be credited in a number of ways **up to a maximum of 12 marks**.*
				
				Depending on the world issue chosen candidates may make reference to any relevant factors, such as:
				• political factors
				• economic factors
				• social factors
				
				Low level of economic development:
				
				Response 1
				Illness and the lack of appropriate medical facilities contribute to the low level of economic development in many parts of Africa. For example, over half a million people die in sub-Saharan Africa each year because of malaria. Malaria reduces the ability to work and save so families cannot meet their needs. In this situation it is difficult for countries to develop their own industries and infrastructure. As a result foreign companies are unwilling to invest or commit their employees to the country. If African governments could provide anti-malaria facilities and equipment then educational attainment would improve and the economy would grow. Such developments however, will take many years to succeed and governments may require foreign aid to do this **(2 marks KU, 2 marks analysis)**.
				
				Arab spring:
				• dissatisfaction with the role of government in a range of countries, including:
				  • protests against dictatorships
				  • lack of human rights
				  • corruption
				• economic issues, including:
				  • economic decline
				  • unemployment
				  • food price rises
				  • extreme poverty
				• social factors, including:
				  • large numbers of disenchanted but highly educated young people
				  • use of social media to inform and spread protests
				
				Any other valid point that meets the criteria described in the general marking principles for this kind of question.

HIGHER MODERN STUDIES
2016

Section 1 — Democracy in Scotland and the United Kingdom

Question	General Marking Instructions for this type of question	Max marks	Specific Marking Instructions for this question
1.	The candidate is required to interpret/evaluate up to three complex sources in order to reach conclusions. In order to achieve credit candidates must show evidence which explains the conclusions reached. Award up to **3 marks** for appropriate use of evidence depending on the quality of the explanation and the synthesis of the evidence to reach any one conclusion. For **full marks** candidates must refer to all sources in their answer. For **full marks** candidates must reach conclusions about each of the points given and make an overall conclusion on the issue.	8	*Candidates can be credited in a number of ways up to a maximum of 8 marks.* **Possible approaches to answering the question:** **The link between government policy and the turnout of different age groups** **Response 1** The turnout of different age groups depends on which group is targeted by the government. Younger voters are less likely to vote (only 43% for youngest group). This has been caused by the government aiming policies at older groups who are much more likely to vote, e.g. 65s and over *(2 marks for synthesis of evidence across Sources A and B with conclusion).* **Response 2** Specific policies like the abolition of the EMA have led to lower turnout by young voters. This stands at 35% less than the oldest age group. This policy may not affect older people directly, whereas the increase in the flat rate pension will benefit many of them greatly. As older people are more likely to vote, government policies are more likely to benefit them which in turn leads to even higher turnouts among the over 65s *(3 marks for synthesis between Sources A, B and C and a conclusion).* **Response 3** Different government policies lead to different turnout rates in different age groups *(0 marks for conclusion with no supporting evidence).* **The link between government policy and the turnout of different socio-economic groups** **Response 4** Different government policies lead to different turnout rates in different socio-economic groups. The wealthiest groups like social classes A and B are most likely to vote *(1 mark for conclusion and correct use of Source A).* **Response 5** Government policies aimed at certain socio-economic groups have a huge effect on the turnout at elections of these groups. For example, those who rent their house either privately or socially are the least likely groups to vote. Those who own their own homes are not affected by government policies like the bedroom tax which will see some benefits removed from those who rent. This means that they will be more likely to vote, as is proven in Source B where home owners have the highest turnout at 77%. As these wealthier groups are more likely to vote then governments will continue to "pass laws which benefit the groups most likely to vote" Source A *(3 marks for conclusion backed by detailed use of sources and synthesis).* **Possible overall conclusion about turnout in the UK** **Response 6** The overall conclusion is that turnout in the UK is increasing *(0 marks for overall conclusion without supporting evidence).*

Question	General Marking Instructions for this type of question	Max marks	Specific Marking Instructions for this question
1.	(continued)		**Response 7** The overall conclusion is that turnout in the UK is increasing. Source B tells me it went from 65.1% in 2010 to 66.1% in 2015 *(1 mark for a valid overall conclusion based on evidence)*. **Response 8** The overall conclusion is that turnout in the UK is increasing. Source B tells me it has steadily increased from 59.4% in 2001 to 66.1% in 2015. There was only a small 1% increase in 2015 largely caused by the massive jump in turnout in Scotland caused by the referendum *(2 marks for a valid overall conclusion based on evidence from two sources)*. **Response 9** Overall, turnout level in UK elections is very uneven between different ages and groups. Older people (65+) are almost twice as likely to vote than younger groups (18–24). Those in more affluent group such as home owners and class A/B are also more likely to vote *(2 marks for a valid overall conclusion based on evidence from two sources)*. **Please note that a valid conclusion which is not supported with relevant source evidence should be given no credit.** *Any other valid point that meets the criteria described in the general marking principles for this kind of question.*
2.	(a)	An analysis mark should be awarded where a candidate uses their knowledge and understanding/a source, to identify relevant components (e.g. of an idea, theory, argument, etc.) and clearly show at least one of the following: • links between different components • links between component(s) and the whole • links between components(s) and related concepts • similarities and contradictions • consistency and inconsistency • different views/interpretations • possible consequences/implications • the relative importance of components • understanding of underling order or structure Up to **8 marks** for KU (description, explanation and exemplification) and up to **4 marks** for analytical comments. Award up to **6 marks** per point Candidates should be credited up to **full marks** if they answer within a Scottish context only, a UK context only or refer to both Scotland and the UK as appropriate. Where a candidate makes more evaluative points than are required to gain the maximum allocation of **4 marks**, these can be credited as knowledge and understanding marks provided they meet the criteria for this.	12	*Candidates can be credited in a number of ways up to a maximum of 12 marks.* **Credit reference to aspects of the following:** *Additional Member System:* • Two votes so more opportunity to choose candidates from a minority group, better representing their views. • The degree of proportionality allows for a wider range of parties to gain representation providing better representation. • Constituency and list representatives gives more choice of representative for voters. • Parties are more easily held to account. • Likelihood of coalition (not recently) forces a wider range of views to be considered. *Balanced by:* • Recent elections show that majority governments can be elected on a minority of the vote due to the FPTP element of AMS. • Coalitions are perhaps not representative as this "compromise" did not appear on the ballot paper. • Two ballot papers could be confusing, increasing voter apathy, lowering turnouts and therefore leading to the underrepresentation of sections of society. • Link between constituency and representative is weakened. *First Past the Post:* • Link between representative and constituency is clear and improves representation of views due to direct accountability. • Usually produces a majority, single party government which can legislate in line with promises without compromise.

Question		General Marking Instructions for this type of question	Max marks	Specific Marking Instructions for this question
2.	(a)	(continued)		*Balanced by:* • In UK elections it has favoured two large parties for many years. In Scotland it exaggerated the representation of the Labour Party for many decades. • Views not well represented due to the creation of many safe seats. • Lack of proportionality between number of votes and number of seats, e.g. 2015 election. • Tactical voting is possible and is often actively encouraged. This means the views of the electorate are not well represented as many vote for candidates they don't actually agree with. *Single Transferable Vote:* • Voters can choose between candidates from within the same party, improving the representation of their views. • The degree of proportionality allows for a wider range of parties to gain representation providing better representation. • Multi-member wards allow voters to select candidates from different parties. • Greater likelihood of coalition in councils forces a wider range of views to be considered. *Balanced by:* • Coalitions are perhaps not representative as this "compromise" did not appear on the ballot paper. • Link between constituency and representative is weakened. *Regional Lists:* • Provides a high degree of proportionality, reflecting voters' views. • Large regions allow parties with "thinly-spread" support to gain representation. *Balanced by:* • Too much power is given to parties to select candidates on the list. • Link between constituency and representative is weakened. *Any other valid point that meets the criteria described in the general marking principles for this type of question.* **Possible approaches to answering the question:** **Response 1** The Scottish Parliament uses the Additional Member System (AMS) to elect 129 MSPs split between 73 constituencies and 8 regional lists *(1 mark KU)*. AMS allows each voter two separate votes, one for their constituency MSP and one for their region, providing better representation for their views *(1 mark analysis)*. (Total 2 marks — 1 mark KU, 1 mark analysis) **Response 2** The Scottish Parliament uses the Additional Member System (AMS) to elect 129 MSPs split between 73 constituencies and 8 regional lists *(1 mark KU)*. Voters have one vote for a constituency MSP and one vote for a regional list MSP which could lead to a higher turnout if voters know their second vote helps elect a regional MSP from the party they support *(1 mark KU, 1 mark analysis)*. The constituency FPTP element of AMS, only allows voters to have one choice for a constituency MSP. This has led to the claim that many votes are "wasted" because with FPTP, only votes for the winning candidate matter. Second-placed candidates get nothing *(1 mark analysis)*. (Total 4 marks — 2 marks KU, 2 marks analysis)

Question		General Marking Instructions for this type of question	Max marks	Specific Marking Instructions for this question
2.	(a)	(continued)		**Response 3** Systems of proportional representation such as the Additional Member System are said to be fairer and provide for better representation of the views of the electorate. Since devolution, Scotland has used AMS to elect the 129 MSPs, a mixture of FPTP to elect constituency MSPs and regional list to elect "top up" MSPs *(1 mark KU)*. Tactical voting is still possible in the First Past the Post constituency ballot, which affects the accuracy of the result but this is balanced by the second ballot which uses a regional list system, creating a more proportional result *(1 mark KU, 1 mark analysis)*. Each voter has a total of 8 MSPs to represent their views. This extra choice allows for more participation and a much higher level of representation. Voters can contact the MSP who best represents their political views *(1 mark KU, 1 mark analysis)*. **(Total 5 marks — 3 marks KU, 2 marks analysis)** **Response 4** First Past the Post is used across the UK to elect 650 MPs to the Westminster Parliament. Each voter selects the candidate they want and whichever one gets the most votes wins the constituency and a seat in parliament. The winner does not need more than 50% of the total vote. In some marginal constituencies the winning candidate may only receive around 30% of the total vote. **(Total — 2 marks KU)** **Response 5** The single transferable vote (STV) system improves the representation of the electorate's views as there is a close relationship between the proportion of votes gained by a party and the number of councillors they win. A PR system like this allows those voters who support smaller parties like the Greens, to confidently vote for them knowing that a simple majority is not required, as it is in the traditionally used First Past the Post system. This proportionality is the main strength of STV and allows the views of voters to be extremely well represented. **(Total 4 marks — 2 marks KU, 2 marks analysis)** *Any other valid point that meets the criteria described in the general marking instructions for this kind of question.*
	(b)	An analysis mark should be awarded where a candidate uses their knowledge and understanding/a source, to identify relevant components (e.g. of an idea, theory, argument, etc.) and clearly show at least one of the following: • links between different components • links between component(s) and the whole • links between components(s) and related concepts • similarities and contradictions • consistency and inconsistency • different views/interpretations • possible consequences/implications • the relative importance of components • understanding of underling order or structure Up to **8 marks** for KU (description, explanation and exemplification) and up to **4 marks** for analytical comments.	12	*Candidates can be credited in a number of ways up to a maximum of 12 marks.* **Credit reference to aspects of the following:** • Ways in which groups in society seek to influence decision making in government • Use of campaigns by groups and organisations designed to impact upon decision making in government, e.g. media campaigns, petitions, lobbying, rallies/demonstrations, etc. • Increase of direct action campaigns — Occupy Movement, Anonymous Organisation, the 99%, Student Protests in England and Wales, Anti-Fracking campaigns, Third Runway and HS2 Opposition • Individual backing of Campaigns by MPs, e.g. Greg Mulholland MP and the Aims of the Campaign for Real Ale (removal of beer duty escalator) Tom Watson MP and anti-hacking campaign • Evidence of very close links between commercial organisations and government, e.g. News International and various governments, Levenson Inquiry and links between PM and senior News Int. execs.

Question		General Marking Instructions for this type of question	Max marks	Specific Marking Instructions for this question
2.	(b)	(continued) Award up to **6 marks** per point Candidates should be credited up to **full marks** if they answer within a Scottish context only, a UK context only or refer to both Scotland and the UK as appropriate. Where a candidate makes more evaluative points than are required to gain the maximum allocation of **4 marks**, these can be credited as knowledge and understanding marks provided they meet the criteria for this.		• Differences between the effect of some groups in influencing decision making than others, e.g. Insider groups/outsider groups. Sectional interest groups exist to promote interests of their members (Trade Unions/CBI). Single Issue groups to promote a particular issue or viewpoint (Stop the War Campaign, Axe the Bedroom Tax) • Voting — more influential in some circumstances, e.g. marginal constituencies • Individual contacting representatives, e.g. surgeries • Influence of the Civil Service on Governmental Decision making • Use of e-petitions to shape Governmental business and discussion • The ways in which some pressure groups use the media to influence decision making through public opinion and their effectiveness • Backing of MPs by trade unions and private businesses. Limit and extent of influence of Trade Unions and private businesses • Use of social media and internet including Twitter, Facebook, Youtube by groups and individuals to galvanise public opinion and influence governmental decision making • Concern of extent and influence of paid lobbyists within House of Lords and the Commons • Proposals for statutory register of lobbyists to identify who they act on behalf of as well as a limit on expenditure by organisations and lobbyists (but excluding Political Parties) during the general election. Concern by charities and academics that the Lobbying Bill could undermine "fabric of democracy" • Allegations of paid relationships between lobbyists and members of House of Lords. Suspension of members of HofL due to closeness to lobbyists and conflict of interest • Ability of MPs, HofLs, Parliamentary Committees in influencing in Government decision making *Any other valid point that meets the criteria described in the general marking instructions for this kind of question.* **Possible approaches to answering this question:** **Response 1** Some commentators and politicians believe that the links between some MPs, Members of the House of Lords and some paid lobbyists are far too close and may harm the democratic process. Some MPs and Lords are paid as consultants for companies and many see this as a conflict of interest between their constituents and the companies that pay them *(1 mark KU, 1 mark analysis)*. **Response 2** The Labour Party is concerned about the number of hedge funds and City of London firms who donate regularly to the Conservative Party and, in return, the Conservatives complain about the link between individual Labour MPs, the Labour Party and the Trade Union movement *(1 mark KU)*. This has led government to introduce proposals for a statutory register of lobbyists and a limit on the amount that organisations can spend during a General Election. Some charities and academics have said that these proposals could undermine the "fabric of democracy". This not just shows that some people are concerned about the effects that lobbyists have on decision making but also that new proposals to limit group's abilities to affect change in government could actually limit decision making and democracy *(2 marks analysis)*. **(Total 5 marks — 2 marks KU, 3 marks analysis)**

Question		General Marking Instructions for this type of question	Max marks	Specific Marking Instructions for this question
2.	(b)	(continued)		**Response 3** Some groups outside of Parliament are more effective than others in influencing Governmental decision making. For example, insider groups can be said to be more successful and effective in influencing government policy than outsider groups. An insider group generally have strong links to the government and are usually regularly asked by the government for their opinion and ideas on areas that they are familiar with. *(1 mark KU, 1 mark analysis)*. Insider groups usually represent a specific interest or section of society, e.g. The British Medical Association (BMA) or Confederation of British Industry. Trade Unions can also be seen as an insider group, for example, the teacher's Union in Scotland, the EIS, is regularly consulted by the Scottish Government over education issues such as the introduction of the Curriculum for Excellence *(2 marks KU)*. **(Total 4 marks — 3 marks KU, 1 mark analysis)** **Response 4** Government may involve insider groups in decision making as they tend to be very knowledgeable about their specific area of interest and as a consequence, government will use their expertise when drafting policies or laws *(1 mark analysis)*. For example, Government sought the advice of the CBI over the proposed increase in the National Minimum Wage as well as when the government were creating new legislation limiting the number of non EU workers doing various types of work in the UK *(2 marks KU)*. However, outsider groups often struggle to make government listen or influence the decisions they make. It may be because the group's demands are not in line with the government's policies. For example, The Stop the War coalition against war in Iraq and Afghanistan demonstrated in London with over a million demonstrators protesting. Despite it being the largest demonstration ever in the UK, the government still went ahead and sent British soldiers to war. Therefore, this shows that some groups are more successful than others with insider groups often being more influential than outsider groups *(1 mark KU, 2 marks analysis)*. **(Total 6 marks — 3 marks KU, 3 marks analysis)**

Section 2 — Social Issues in the United Kingdom

Part A: Social inequality in the United Kingdom

Question	General Marking Instructions for this type of question	Max marks	Specific Marking Instructions for this question
3. (a)	An analysis mark should be awarded where a candidate uses their knowledge and understanding/a source, to identify relevant components (e.g. of an idea, theory, argument, etc.) and clearly show at least one of the following: • links between different components • links between component(s) and the whole • links between components(s) and related concepts • similarities and contradictions • consistency and inconsistency • different views/interpretations • possible consequences/implications • the relative importance of components • understanding of underling order or structure Evaluation involves making a judgments based on criteria, drawing conclusions on the extent to which a view is supported by the evidence; counter-arguments including possible alternative interpretations; the overall impact/significance of the factors when taken together; the relative importance of factors in relation to the context. Credit responses that make reference to: • Government policies • Analysis/evaluation of the impact that these policies have had on reducing inequalities • Balanced overall evaluative comment on the effectiveness of government policies in reducing inequalities • Provide a clear, coherent line of argument **General Marking Instructions** Candidates should be credited up to full marks if they answer within a Scottish context only, a UK context only or refer to both Scotland and the UK as appropriate. Up to **8 marks** for KU (description, explanation and exemplification) and up to **12 marks** for analytical/ evaluative comments. Award up to **6 marks** per point. Where a candidate makes more analytical/evaluative points than are required to gain the maximum allocation of 8 marks, these can be credited as knowledge and understanding marks provided they meet the criteria for this.	20	Government policies have failed to reduce social inequalities. Discuss. *Candidates can be credited in a number of ways up to a maximum of 20 marks.* **Credit reference to aspects of the following:** • Recent government policies • Analysis/evaluation of the impact that these policies have had on reducing inequalities • Balanced overall evaluative comment on the effectiveness of government policies in reducing inequalities • Provide a clear, coherent line of argument Wide range of Welfare State provision including State benefits, healthcare, education, housing and personal/ children's social services, employment services. • Debate over access, quality and extent of State support including introduction of means-testing of Child Benefit, tightening of benefit rules, etc. The removal of some universal benefits. Under-26s unable to claim housing benefit. • Equalities legislation including Equality Act 2012 as well as The Commission for Equality and Human Rights; Gender Equality Duty Code of Practice; Women's Enterprise Task Force. • The introduction of the Universal Credit, cap on benefit limits, "bedroom tax", etc. • Credit candidates who make reference to/comment on Scottish government policies, e.g. end of prescription charges, free personal care for the elderly, etc. • Previous government policies — Tax Credits system, National Minimum Wage, work of equal value, changes in maternity and paternity leave arrangements. • Reference to official reports, e.g. poverty levels among pensioners and children, unemployment statistics, statistics on inequalities by socioeconomic group, gender, race, etc. Stats may cover income, wealth, education and health outcomes, etc. • Poverty reduction targets (children, fuel poverty) not being met but some progress being made, e.g. just under 20% of children (2.3m) lived in households classed as below poverty line in 2012 a drop of 2% or 300,000 children from year before. Numbers in severe poverty also fell. Child poverty groups claim figure is higher, nearer 4m or more than 1 in 4 of all children. CPAG claims figure will rise in future as cap on benefits and bedroom tax begin to hit the poorest sections of society. • The poorest 10% of population have, on average, seen a fall in their real incomes after deducting housing costs, changes in benefits, etc. The richest 10% have seen bigger proportional rises in their income than any other group. There is growing evidence of inequality between the very rich and the very poor within UK. The UK's Gini Co-efficient is rising and higher than any point in last thirty years. OECD claims inequality rising faster in UK than any other rich nation. • Gender pay gap: UK women in full time work earn 10% less per hour (2012). Gender pay gap is bigger for part time work. Four in five paid carers are women. The care sector's poor pay contributes greatly to the gender pay gap. However, pay gap narrowing in some areas of employment.

Question		General Marking Instructions for this type of question	Max marks	Specific Marking Instructions for this question
3.	(a)	(continued)		• Women make up 60% of the university population; success of women in reaching senior posts varies from place to place. "Glass ceiling" only cracked, not broken. • Women make up 29% of MPs (Increased from 22% in 2010); 19% of directors in FTSE 100 firms are women (increased from 12% in 2010) despite accounting for over 46% of the labour force. • Unemployment is higher amongst minority groups; far higher for 18–24 year olds; employment rates for ethnic minority groups lower but gap narrowing. • There is growing evidence of a "race pay gap". Women from Black Caribbean, Pakistani and Bangladeshi groups most likely to face a higher risk of unemployment, lower pay and have fewer prospects for promotion. • Any other valid point. *Any other valid point that meets the criteria described in the general marking instructions for this kind of question.* **Possible approaches to answering this question:** **Response 1** Governments have introduced various laws and policies to help to try and tackle some inequalities in the UK. These laws and policies include the Equality Act 2010, Working Tax Credits or the National Minimum Wage *(1 mark KU)*. **Response 2** Some people argue that changes in the benefits system made by the Coalition government led to growing inequalities and increased poverty for some sections of society particularly the low paid and those receiving benefits *(1 mark analysis)*. The Coalition Govt. cut the benefits budget as part of their austerity programme following the world recession. This has led to many of the poorest people in the UK being worse off as some benefits were scrapped and new changes introduced. The creation of Universal Credit, the "Bedroom tax" and limits on the amount of benefits that people receive has created further hardship for some families and may have may even have increased child poverty *(1 mark KU, 1 mark analysis, 1 mark evaluative comment)*. However, government policies have also indirectly benefited some groups. The National Minimum wage has benefited 2 million workers with 75% of these being women and ethnic minorities. However, many feel that the levels of the minimum wage are too low and are campaigning for a Living Wage increase to this policy. This shows that the policy has benefited people but that it also doesn't go far enough to fully tackle some inequalities *(1 mark KU, 1 mark evaluative comment)*. **(Total 7 marks — 2 marks KU, 2 marks analysis, 2 marks evaluative comment)** **Response 3** Despite legislation such as the 2010 Equality Act making it illegal for employers to discriminate against someone on the basis of gender, race, religion, sexuality, etc., discrimination still takes place. For example, 30,000 women every year are forced to leave their job every year due to pregnancy *(1 mark KU, 1 mark analysis)*. This shows that even with laws in place, discrimination does still happen. Men may earn around 18% more than women but the gap between male and female earnings is getting smaller and this demonstrates that the "pay gap" between men and women is improving but there is a long way to go before women and men achieve pay equality *(1 mark KU, 1 mark evaluative comment)*. **(Total 4 marks — 2 marks KU, 1 mark analysis, 1 mark evaluation)**

Question	General Marking Instructions for this type of question	Max marks	Specific Marking Instructions for this question
3. (a)	(continued)		**Response 4** Despite the introduction of the Equality Act, discrimination still exists but many women are now obtaining high status jobs in companies and organisations, for example, over 60% of HR directors in the City of London are female but only occupy 30% of managing director positions. **(Total 2 marks — 1 mark KU, 1 mark evaluation)**
(b)	An analysis mark should be awarded where a candidate uses their knowledge and understanding/a source, to identify relevant components (e.g. of an idea, theory, argument, etc.) and clearly show at least one of the following: • links between different components • links between component(s) and the whole • links between components(s) and related concepts • similarities and contradictions • consistency and inconsistency • different views/interpretations • possible consequences/implications • the relative importance of components • understanding of underling order or structure Evaluation involves making judgements based on criteria, drawing conclusions on the extent to which a view is supported by the evidence; counter-arguments including possible alternative interpretations; the overall impact/significance of the factors when taken together; the relative importance of factors in relation to the context. Credit responses that make reference to: • Theories of the causes of crime • Analysis of the importance of human nature as the main cause of crime • Balanced overall evaluative comment on the importance of human nature as the main cause of crime • Provide a clear, coherent line of argument Up to **8 marks** for KU (description, explanation and exemplification) and up to **12 marks** for analytical/evaluative comments. Award up to **6 marks** per point. Candidates should be credited up to **full marks** if they answer within a Scottish context only, a UK context only or refer to both Scotland and the UK as appropriate. Where a candidate makes more analytical/evaluative points than are required to gain the maximum allocation of **4 marks**, these can be credited as knowledge and understanding marks provided they meet the criteria for this.	20	*Candidates can be credited in a number of ways up to a maximum of 20 marks.* **Credit reference to aspects of the following:** • Poor lifestyle choices include smoking, excess alcohol consumption, lack of exercise, a diet high in salt and fat, drug misuse, or other risk-taking activities • Failure to make best use of preventative care services • Reference to government policies or health initiatives where it is acknowledged that these are a response to poor lifestyle choices, e.g. minimum alcohol pricing • Reference to official reports, e.g. Equally Well 2008 (and Inequalities Task Force Report 2010) • Statistical examples that highlight poor health in Scotland and/or the UK, e.g. the big five *Any other valid point that meets the criteria described in the general marking principles for this kind of question.* **Possible approaches to answering the question:** **Response 1** Some people choose to drink too much alcohol. Scotland has a culture of binge drinking especially at the weekend which costs the country a great deal of money *(1 mark KU)*. **Response 2** Poor diet is a problem in Scottish society. Many people choose to eat too much fatty food such as burgers and chips. Health campaigns such as the 5-a-day campaign to encourage people to eat more fruit and vegetables are a response to too many people choosing to eat a poor diet *(2 marks KU)*. **Response 3** Despite years of anti-smoking health campaigns or the ban on smoking in public places, some individuals continue to choose to smoke cigarettes. Around 22% of adults smoked in Scotland in 2012 *(1 mark KU, 1 mark analysis)*. As a consequence of smoking an individual is more likely to suffer from respiratory illness or lung cancer. Around 90% of all lung cancer deaths are linked to people who smoked before they died. Therefore it is clear that lifestyle choices have a massive impact on health *(1 mark KU, 1 mark evaluation)*. **(Total 4 marks — 2 marks KU, 1 mark analysis, 1 mark evaluation)** **Response 4** There are many lifestyle choices that can be made to improve health. People can choose not to smoke, drink too much alcohol or eat too much fatty food *(1 mark KU)*. Statistics show that Scotland has many people who make the wrong lifestyle choices, e.g. around one in five adults smoke *(1 mark KU)*. Choosing to take regular exercise is another important way that people can stay fit and healthy. Walking or cycling to school or work regularly has been proven to improve people's health. Many people in Scotland don't take regular exercise.

Question		General Marking Instructions for this type of question	Max marks	Specific Marking Instructions for this question
3.	(b)	(continued)		Studies show that less than half the adult population takes an hour's exercise at least three times per week (**2 marks KU**). In Scotland the government has tried to tackle ill-health by encouraging people to take more exercise however the people that have taken up the opportunities are more often the affluent rather than the poorest. Despite the Equally Well Report of 2008 recognising that there was a need to promote exercise there is still a clear need for Scotland to make better lifestyle choices to improve health (**2 marks analysis**).
				(Total 6 marks — 4 marks KU, 2 marks analysis)
				Response 5 Overall, it is clear that lifestyle choices have a huge impact on an individual's health. However, what is also clear is that an individual's economic position will influence these choices. A healthy diet or a gym membership, are both more affordable for the middle classes who are more likely to have a comfortable income. Not all middle class people will make the healthy choice but they are more likely to as they have the finance to make that option possible. A single parent who relies on benefits may know which choice is healthy and may want to make that choice but will be forced to make a different choice due to finance. It is too simplistic to blame individuals for "making bad choices" without taking their financial position into consideration.
				(Total 3 marks evaluation)

Part B: Crime and the law in the United Kingdom

Question		General Marking Instructions for this type of question	Max marks	Specific Marking Instructions for this question
3.	(c)	An analysis mark should be awarded where a candidate uses their knowledge and understanding/a source, to identify relevant components (e.g. of an idea, theory, argument, etc.) and clearly show at least one of the following: • links between different components • links between component(s) and the whole • links between components(s) and related concepts • similarities and contradictions • consistency and inconsistency • different views/interpretations • possible consequences/implications • the relative importance of components • understanding of underling order or structure Evaluation involves making a judgments based on criteria, drawing conclusions on the extent to which a view is supported by the evidence; counter-arguments including possible alternative interpretations; the overall impact/ significance of the factors when taken together; the relative importance of factors in relation to the context.	20	*Candidates can be credited in a number of ways **up to a maximum of 20 marks**.* **Credit reference to aspects of the following:** The Scottish government has introduced or extended a range of policies to reduce crime or improve crime prevention including: • policies to tackle antisocial behaviour • policies on counteracting the threat of terrorism • drugs — recovery and enforcement • new laws give greater protection to victims of forced marriage • tougher sanctions on crime linked to racial, religious or social prejudice • action on human trafficking • tough enforcement and prevention measures • protecting children from exploitation and dealing with extreme materials • policies on tackling prostitution and kerb-crawling offences • reducing re-offending • tackling serious organised crime in Scotland • reforming rape and sexual offences law • tackling misuse of firearms and air weapons in Scotland • youth justice measures — early intervention and tackling youth crime • introducing specialist drug courts • community payback orders • restriction of liberty orders • creation of Police Scotland Measures to implement some of the above were contained in the Criminal Justice and Licensing (Scotland) Act 2010.

Question		General Marking Instructions for this type of question	Max marks	Specific Marking Instructions for this question
3.	**(c)**	(continued) Credit responses that make reference to: • Theories of the causes of crime • Analysis of the importance of human nature as the main cause of crime • Balanced overall evaluative comment on the importance of human nature as the main cause of crime • Provide a clear, coherent line of argument Up to **8 marks** for KU (description, explanation and exemplification) and up to **12 marks** for analytical/ evaluative comments. Award up to **6 marks** per point. Candidates should be credited up to **full marks** if they answer within a Scottish context only, a UK context only or refer to both Scotland and the UK as appropriate. Where a candidate makes more analytical/evaluative points than are required to gain the maximum allocation of **4 marks**, these can be credited as knowledge and understanding marks provided they meet the criteria for this.		In England and Wales, the Home Office claims emphasis is moving towards local community-based approaches to reducing crime, including improving crime prevention: • creating community triggers to deal with persistent antisocial behaviour • using community safety partnerships, and police and crime commissioners, • to work out local approaches to deal with issues, including antisocial behaviour, drug or alcohol misuse and re-offending • establishing the national referral mechanism (NRM) to make it easier for all the different agencies that could be involved in a trafficking case to co operate, share information about potential victims and access advice, accommodation and support • setting up the National Crime Agency (NCA) which will be a new body of operational crime fighters • creating street-level crime maps to give the public up-to-date, accurate information on what is happening on their streets so they can challenge the police on performance • creating the child sex offender disclosure scheme, which allows anyone concerned about a child to find out if someone in their life has a record for child sexual offences • legislating against hate crime • using football banning orders to stop potential trouble-makers from travelling to football matches both at home and abroad • legislation to prohibit cash payments to buy scrap metal and reforming the regulation of the scrap metal industry to stop unscrupulous dealers buying stolen metal The Antisocial Behaviour, Crime and Policing Bill was announced in May 2013. It aims to tackle a number of types of crime including antisocial behaviour, illegal use of firearms and organised crime. References can be made to Scottish and/or UK-based crime reduction policies. *Any other valid point that meets the criteria described in the general marking principles for this kind of question.* **Possible approaches to answering the question:** **Response 1** To try and reduce crime in Scotland the Scottish government has announced it will increase the mandatory sentence for carrying a knife from four to five years. The Scottish government hopes this will stop young people carrying knives *(1 mark KU)*. **Response 2** In Scotland there are many early intervention programmes that have been introduced to try and reduce crime. One early intervention programme is 'Kick It Kick Off' (KIKO) *(1 mark KU)*. This programme uses football to try and steer young people, many who have had problems at school or with the police, away from trouble *(1 mark KU)*. KIKO has reduced crime by providing a safe alternative to gang activity for many young Scots *(1 mark analysis)*. **(Total 3 marks — 2 marks KU, 1 mark analysis)**

Question		General Marking Instructions for this type of question	Max marks	Specific Marking Instructions for this question
3.	(c)	(continued)		**Response 3** The Criminal Justice and Licensing (Scotland) Act 2010 strengthened the law in terms of racial or religiously motivated crime. Now, where it has been proved that someone has committed an offence on grounds of race or religion (hate crimes), the courts must take this into account when handing out the sentence. This can lead to a longer custodial sentence or higher fine or a different type of punishment where appropriate *(3 marks KU)*. Although many people support tougher punishments for hate crimes, arguing this will make some people think twice before committing a crime, there are those who believe longer or tougher sentencing is the wrong approach. These people would argue that there is little evidence tougher sentencing for hate crimes works *(2 marks analysis)*. **(Total 5 marks — 3 marks KU, 2 marks analysis)**
	(d)	An analysis mark should be awarded where a candidate uses their knowledge and understanding/a source, to identify relevant components (e.g. of an idea, theory, argument, etc.) and clearly show at least one of the following: • links between different components • links between component(s) and the whole • links between components(s) and related concepts • similarities and contradictions • consistency and inconsistency • different views/interpretations • possible consequences/implications • the relative importance of components • understanding of underling order or structure Evaluation involves making a judgments based on criteria, drawing conclusions on the extent to which a view is supported by the evidence; counter-arguments including possible alternative interpretations; the overall impact/significance of the factors when taken together; the relative importance of factors in relation to the context. Credit responses that make reference to: • Theories of the causes of crime • Analysis of the importance of human nature as the main cause of crime • Balanced overall evaluative comment on the importance of human nature as the main cause of crime • Provide a clear, coherent line of argument Up to **8 marks** for KU (description, explanation and exemplification) and up to **12 marks** for analytical/evaluative comments.	20	*Candidates can be credited in a number of ways up to a maximum of 20 marks.* **Credit reference to aspects of the following:** • Human nature theory • Robert Merton/Strain theory of crime • Cultural deviance theory • Marxist theory • Charles Moore/Underclass theory • Conservative social breakdown theory • Reference to links between factors such as, drug/alcohol abuse, peer influence, family influence, etc. which don't mention theorists specifically should still be credited *Any other valid point that meets the criteria described in the general marking instructions for this kind of question.* **Possible approaches to answering this question:** **Response 1** There are many theories as to why people commit crimes; the individualist human nature theory is just one. For example, some people believe in Hobbes's belief that human nature explains crime; we are all essentially selfish and will break the law if given the chance. This could explain looting which took place during the 2011 London riots *(2 marks KU)*. **Response 2** There are many theories as to why people commit crimes; the individualist human nature theory is just one. For example, some people believe in Hobbes's belief that human nature explains crime; we are all essentially selfish and will break the law if given the chance. This could explain looting which took place during the 2011 London riots *(2 marks KU)*. This, however, cannot explain why many people chose not to take part in looting. Indeed, many people chose not to pursue their own self-interest instead they chose to help those whose shops were being looted so there are limits to the individualist human nature theory *(1 mark evaluative comment, 1 mark analysis)*. **(Total 4 marks — 2 marks KU, 1 mark analysis, 1 mark evaluation)**

Question		General Marking Instructions for this type of question	Max marks	Specific Marking Instructions for this question
3.	**(d)**	(continued) Award up to **6 marks** per point. Candidates should be credited up to **full marks** if they answer within a Scottish context only, a UK context only or refer to both Scotland and the UK as appropriate. Where a candidate makes more analytical/evaluative points than are required to gain the maximum allocation of **4 marks**, these can be credited as knowledge and understanding marks provided they meet the criteria for this.		**Response 3** There are many theories of as to why people commit crimes; the individualist human nature theory is just one. For example, some people believe in Hobbes's belief that human nature explains crime; we are all essentially selfish and will break the law if given the chance. This could explain looting which took place during the 2011 London riots *(2 marks KU)*. Another explanation would be a Marxist explanation which believes that inequalities in society can explain crime. Those who are excluded from power and wealth will not respect the law and will commit crime. Evidence from the London riots showed that it was mostly people who were unemployed or "NEETs" who took part *(2 marks KU)*. Neither of these theories though can explain why some people choose not to commit crimes. Not everyone took part in the London riot looting and not all people from poor backgrounds are criminals. This suggests that other factors must play an important part in determining who will and who won't commit crime *(1 mark analysis, 1 mark evaluative comment)*. **(Total 6 marks — 4 marks KU, 1 mark analysis, 1 mark evaluation)** **Response 4** Some theories overlap in their explanations of the causes of crime. Charles Moore blames the growing "underclass" who he claims choose to live off benefits and have no stake in society, therefore do not care about obeying the law. This is an individualist view but a Marxist would also agree that capitalism from time to time creates a group of people who are marginalised. Human nature is not the sole cause; it is the economic system which creates criminals. **(Total 3 marks — 1 mark KU, 1 mark analysis, 1 mark evaluation)** **Response 5** Overall, there are many different theories of crime, each with their strengths and weaknesses. Some theories, such as social breakdown, are good at explaining crimes relating to gangs and drug use. But this theory has little to say about crimes committed by the better off in society. Marxist theories are better at explaining corporate crime but are weaker at explaining why some individuals choose not to commit crime. In conclusion, it would seem to be fair to say that human nature plays some part in explaining crime but does not explain why certain groups in society are more likely than others to be involved in crime. A complex mixture of social and economic factors is responsible for the criminal behaviour, or lack of it, shown by each individual *(4 marks evaluation)*.

Section 3 — International Issues

Question	General Marking Instructions for this type of question	Max marks	Specific Marking Instructions for this question
4.	The candidate is required to interpret/evaluate up to three complex sources of information detecting and explaining the extent of objectivity. In order to achieve credit candidates must show evidence which supports the extent of accuracy in a given viewpoint. Award up to 3 marks for: • appropriate use of evidence depending on the quality of the explanation and the synthesis of the evidence for any one explanation of the extent of objectivity. • For **full marks** candidates must refer to all sources in their answer. • For **full marks** candidates must make an overall judgment as to the extent of the accuracy of the given statement. • accuracy of the statement. Award up to **3 marks** for: • appropriate use of evidence depending on the quality of the explanation and the synthesis of the evidence for any one explanation of the extent of objectivity. • For **full marks** candidates must refer to all sources in their answer. • For **full marks** candidates must make an overall judgment as to the extent of the accuracy of the given statement. • accuracy of the statement. • Candidates may be awarded up to a maximum of **2 marks** for incorporating an evaluation of the reliability of the sources in their explanations although this is not mandatory. Maximum of **6 marks** if no overall judgement made on extent of accuracy.	8	*Candidates can be credited in a number of ways **up to a maximum of 8 marks.*** **Evidence that supports the view ("*Russia effectively protects the rights of its citizens*")** Examples of the types of evidence that support the view include: • Source C, there has been an extension of jury trials across the country • Source C, the death penalty has been suspended • Source A, no executions since 1996 • Source C, fewer complaints, drop from 58,000 to 24,000 in two years • Source C, right of protest is protected by law • Source A, campaign groups had the freedom to challenge the law in the courts • Source B, better rights than China or Saudi Arabia **Response 1** The rights of Russians are well protected as in Source A campaign groups could take the government to court, which is an important right. This is supported by Source C which states that the right to protest is protected and that registering as a foreign agent did not affect this right *(2 marks, evidence linked from two sources).* **Evidence that opposes the view ("*Russia effectively protects the rights of its citizens*")** • Source A, groups forced to register as "foreign agents" which is seen as traitor by Russian people • Source A, media campaign to discredit groups • Source A, wide definition means a large number of campaign groups can be included • Source A, leaders prosecuted and groups with no option but to disband • Source A, court decision supports government, many complain about courts (56% Source C) • Source B, Russia compares badly to other major countries in Political Rights index meaning poor freedom of speech, participation, etc.(backed by information from Source A) • Source B, Russia rating on the PRI has decreased since 1997, meaning rights are not well protected **Response 2** The rights of Russians are not effectively protected by the government as Russia's rating (Source B) is the second lowest it could be. It has also been in decline from 3 to 6 in recent years. This shows that the right to participate and freedom of speech are not adequately protected. This is supported by Source A which shows that anyone campaigning for improvements has effectively been discredited as a foreign spy by the government. The right to protest may be protected by law (Source C) but this won't be effective if the public are against "Foreign Agents" *(3 marks, relevant evidence from all three sources with evaluative comment).* *Candidates may also be credited **up to 2 marks** on any comment/analysis of the origin and reliability of the source.*

Question	General Marking Instructions for this type of question	Max marks	Specific Marking Instructions for this question
4.	(continued)		Although Source C is fairly up to date (2014) it is unreliable as it comes from Sputniknews.com which is owned and operated by the Russian government and so will present information in a biased way to make them look better **(2 marks)**. • Source A is unreliable as it is adapted **(1 mark)**. • Source A is unreliable as it is adapted. We have no idea how much of this article has been adapted. We also have no idea who adapted it therefore we cannot be sure that it accurately reflects the views of the Human Rights watch group **(2 marks)**. • Statistics in Source B are up to date (2015) **(0 marks)**. • Statistics in Source B are up to date (2015) and so give a fairly up to date picture of the position of Russia compared to other countries **(1 mark)**. • Source C is unreliable as it is adapted. We have no idea how much of this article has been adapted. We also have no idea who adapted it therefore we cannot be sure that it accurately reflects the views of the original author **(2 marks)**. *For full marks, candidates must make an overall judgment as to the extent of the accuracy of the given statement.* **Accept overall judgements similar to:** • On the whole, the evidence suggests that Russia does not protect the rights of its citizens **(0 marks)**. • The statement is largely untrue as the government have made it very difficult for any campaign groups to operate. This means that opposition to their policies is being silenced. Although jury trials are more widespread and there have been no executions since 1996, basic political rights are being denied. The Political Rights Index supports this conclusion as Russia's rating is declining over time and is only better than China and Saudi Arabia **(2 marks)**. • Russia is doing well with Human Rights as the EU praised them for not executing anyone recently **(1 mark)**. • The statement is true to a certain extent, as there have been fewer complaints recently but they rank poorly on the political rights index **(1 mark)**. • The statement is true to a certain extent **(0 marks)**.

Part A: World Powers

Question		General Marking Instructions for this type of question	Max marks	Specific Marking Instructions for this question
5.	(a)	Evaluation involves making judgments, drawing conclusions on the extent to which a view is supported by the evidence; the relative importance of factors; counter-arguments including possible alternative interpretations; the overall impact/significance of the factors when taken together; the relative importance of factors in relation to the context.	12	*Candidates can be credited in a number of ways **up to a maximum of 12 marks**.* **World Power Choice: Brazil** **Possible approaches to answering the question:** **Response 1** Within Brazil there is a widening gap between rich and poor with currently 16 million Brfazilians experiencing poverty and living on less than $44 a month *(1 mark KU)*. One key policy to tackle growing poverty is through the welfare strategy of the Bolsa Familia which provides financial support to those families with children living below the poverty line *(1 mark KU)*. The programme has grown rapidly and in the past ten years, the number of families receiving payments has risen from 3.6 million to 13.8 million covering nearly a quarter of Brazil's population *(1 mark KU)*.

Question		General Marking Instructions for this type of question	Max marks	Specific Marking Instructions for this question
5.	(a)	(continued) Credit responses that make reference to: • Role of world power in international relations • Evaluation of the importance of world power in international relations Up to **8 marks** for KU (description, explanation and exemplification) and up to **4 marks** for evaluative comments. Award up to **6 marks** per point. Where a candidate makes more evaluative points than are required to gain the maximum allocation of **4 marks**, these can be credited as knowledge and understanding marks provided they meet the criteria for this.		However, the payment is conditional and is only guaranteed if the children are kept in school and get vaccinated. Some also argue the payment is too little to live on with payments of 70 reis a person to any family below the poverty line of 140 reis a month, hence not really helping end poverty *(2 marks evaluation)*. Furthermore, some Brazilians have reported that they have tried to claim the benefits paid out by Bolsa Familia and have failed to receive any money from the Government. Critics claim that this policy has had limited success and non-payment is often down to the corruption of local officials *(1 mark KU, 1 mark evaluation)*. **(Total 7 marks — 4 marks KU, 3 marks evaluation)** **Response 2** The number of American citizens without private healthcare insurance or employer-based coverage has increased with currently 47 million people uninsured. The numbers of uninsured Americans increased as access to healthcare became increasingly unaffordable and many employers were reducing the coverage they provided to workers. To assist the 15% of the population who are currently not covered by their employers or by US healthcare programs such as Medicaid, Barack Obama introduced the healthcare reform law which aims to extend health coverage to those who do not have it at a more affordable rate *(3 marks KU)*. Since The Affordable Health Care Act was introduced on October 1st 2013, over 1 million people are estimated to have signed up however, this is a lower up take than expected, showing the policy has had limited success *(1 mark KU, 1 mark evaluation)*. **(Total 5 marks — 4 marks KU, 1 mark evaluation)** **Response 3** The plan to make all Americans take out health care has proved controversial and sign up rates have differed across the states with many Republicans claiming it could end up being very expensive for individuals and firms. Healthcare reform has generated heated debate in the USA as many Republicans worry it will lead to tax increases that are unnecessary, leading to inevitable failure of the policy *(1 mark KU, 2 marks evaluation)*. However, the act is showing encouraging signs of success as people who have pre-existing conditions who previously would have experienced difficulty obtaining coverage, are now covered under the new proposals of 'Obamacare' *(1 mark KU, 1 mark evaluation)*. **(Total 5 marks — 2 marks KU, 3 marks evaluation)**
	(b)	Evaluation involves making judgments, drawing conclusions on the extent to which a view is supported by the evidence; the relative importance of factors; counter-arguments including possible alternative interpretations; the overall impact/significance of the factors when taken together; the relative importance of factors in relation to the context. Credit responses that make reference to: • Role of world power in international relations • Evaluation of the importance of world power in international relations	12	*Candidates can be credited in a number of ways up to a maximum of 12 marks.* Depending on the world power chosen, candidates may make reference to any relevant aspects, such as: • nature of political system • extent of democracy • constitutional arrangements • opportunities to form, join, campaign for political parties • role of electoral system • extent of human and political rights • role of media • opportunities to take part in pressure group/interest group activities

Question	General Marking Instructions for this type of question	Max marks	Specific Marking Instructions for this question
5. (b)	(continued) Up to **8 marks** for KU (description, explanation and exemplification) and up to **4 marks** for evaluative comments. Award up to **6 marks** per point. Where a candidate makes more evaluative points than are required to gain the maximum allocation of **4 marks**, these can be credited as knowledge and understanding marks provided they meet the criteria for this.		**In the USA:** **Response 1** Citizens have a wide range of opportunities to put forward their views. One way of having your views represented is through voting for elected officials. The US Constitution guarantees the right to vote for a large range of political offices including the President of the USA, both houses of Congress and a wide range of state and local officials. Competing parties present candidates for all these positions, voters have a free choice. Although there are many opportunities for US citizens to express their views through voting, turnout in elections, especially at state and county levels, is often low. This may be because many people (especially ethnic minority groups) believe their views will not be represented. **(Total 4 marks — 2 marks KU, 2 marks evaluation)** **In China:** **Response 2** In theory, China is a multi-party socialist state. In the highest bodies of the Chinese government, nine political parties are represented, including the Communist party. However, the views of Chinese citizens are not well-represented as the Communist party is by far the largest party and the other eight parties are only allowed to operate by permission of the CPC and will not disagree or act as an opposition to the views of the CPC. It is also the case that Chinese citizens are not allowed to vote directly for the higher bodies in the political system as the higher bodies are chosen by the body below. Chinese citizens only have the right to directly elect representatives at the very lowest "village" level, which has only limited influence over local issues. **(Total 6 marks — 3 marks KU, 3 marks evaluation)** **In South Africa:** **Response 3** Since the end of apartheid, all citizens have had the right to vote and there are a wide range of political parties which South Africans can choose from. Over the last 20 years, many new political parties have been formed, showing that there are opportunities for different views to be represented. In 2014, the fifth election was held since the end of apartheid and which allows all South Africans to vote. Elections are held every five years for the National Assembly and the provincial legislatures. The African National Congress is the main party in South Africa and it won over 60% of the vote. All the other parties received fewer votes, with the Democratic Alliance receiving just over 20% of the vote and the newly formed Economic Freedom Fighters receiving just over 6% of the vote. **(Total 4 marks — 3 marks KU, 1 mark evaluation)** *Any other valid point that meets the criteria described in the general marking principles for this kind of question.*

Part B: World Issues

Question		General Marking Instructions for this type of question	Max marks	Specific Marking Instructions for this question
5.	(c)	Evaluation involves making judgments based on criteria, drawing conclusions on the extent to which a view is supported by the evidence; counter-arguments including possible alternative interpretations; the overall impact/significance of the factors when taken together; the relative importance of factors in relation to the context. Credit responses that make reference to: • A significant international issue • An evaluation of the impact of the issue on different groups in different countries Up to **8 marks** for KU (description, explanation and exemplification) and up to **4 marks** for evaluative comments. Award up to **6 marks** per point. Candidates may make reference to any world issues the impact which extends beyond the boundaries of any single country. This impact may be regional or global in scale. Where a candidate makes more evaluative points than are required to gain the maximum allocation of **4 marks**, these can be credited as knowledge and understanding marks provided they meet the criteria for this.	12	*Candidates can be credited in a number of ways up to a maximum of 12 marks.* **Credit reference to aspects of the following:** • war — Afghanistan, Libya, Syria • nuclear weapons — North Korea • borders — Middle East • economic difficulties — EU countries (Portugal, Ireland, Italy, Greece, Spain) • factors which limit development *Any other valid point that meets the criteria described in the general marking instructions for this kind of question.* **Possible approaches to answering this question:** **Response 1** The Israeli-Palestine conflict has been going on for a long time. The conflict involves both sides recognising each other as a country and agreeing on which territories, e.g. Jerusalem should belong to Israel or a Palestine state *(1 mark KU).* **Response 2** The Israeli-Palestine conflict has been going on for a long time. The conflict involves both sides recognising each other as a country and agreeing on which territories, e.g. Jerusalem should belong to Israel or a Palestine state. The conflict has resulted in around 16,000 people being killed, the majority of these are Palestinians *(2 marks KU).* The Israeli economy fails to attract foreign investment due to this conflict which seriously hinders economic growth and leads to a much lower standard of living for its people. However, this problem is far more severe for the Palestinians who live in the Gaza Strip who are often forced to rely on foreign aid for survival *(1 mark KU, 2 marks evaluation).* (Total 5 marks — 3 marks KU, 2 marks evaluation) **Response 3** The areas known as "the West Bank" and the Gaza strip are the two most disputed areas in the conflict. The Palestinians refer to this as Occupied Palestinian Territory whereas the Israelis say these are "disputed territories" as no one owned them when Israel captured them in 1967 *(2 marks KU).* The Gaza Strip which is only 25km long has very high levels of poverty and unemployment *(1 mark evaluation).* Israel blockaded the Gaza Strip in 2007 in order to curb the influence of the political group Hamas. Israel maintains the blockade has at no point caused a humanitarian crisis but aid agencies have criticised the conditions people have had to live in, in particular water supplies and toilet conditions *(1 mark KU, 1 mark evaluation).* It is clear that innocent people are suffering in these two areas. As well as many violent deaths, health and education services are badly hampered leading to a great deal of avoidable suffering and an inability to create prosperity through investment and growth *(1 mark KU, 1 mark evaluation).* (Total 7 marks — 4 marks KU, 3 marks evaluation)

Question		General Marking Instructions for this type of question	Max marks	Specific Marking Instructions for this question
5.	(d)	Evaluation involves making judgments based on criteria, drawing conclusions on the extent to which a view is supported by the evidence; counter-arguments including possible alternative interpretations; the overall impact/significance of the factors when taken together; the relative importance of factors in relation to the context. Credit responses that make reference to: • Ways in which international organisations can address a significant world issue • An evaluation of the effectiveness of international organisations in addressing a significant world issue Up to **8 marks** for KU (description, explanation and exemplification) and up to **4 marks** for evaluative comments. Award up to **6 marks** per point. Candidates may make reference to any world issues the impact which extends beyond the boundaries of any single country. This impact may be regional or global in scale. Where a candidate makes more evaluative points than are required to gain the maximum allocation of **4 marks**, these can be credited as knowledge and understanding marks provided they meet the criteria for this.	12	*Candidates can be credited in a number of ways **up to a maximum of 12 marks**.* • World Issue: international terrorism (UN/NATO) • World Issue: developing world poverty (UN agencies/ NGOs) • World Issue: nuclear proliferation (UN) • World Issue: global economic crisis (EU/World Bank/IMF) *Any other valid point that meets the criteria described in the general marking instructions for this kind of question.* **Possible approaches to answering this question: (Terrorism/NATO)** **Response 1** NATO has been involved in the Afghanistan war since 2001. This was an attempt to rid the country of the al Qaeda and the Taliban after the attacks on 9/11 *(1 mark KU)*. **Response 2** NATO has been involved in the Afghanistan war since 2001. This was an attempt to rid the country of al Qaeda and the Taliban after the attacks on 9/11 *(1 mark KU)*. This was the first time NATO had been involved in a conflict in Asia and Operation ISAF attempted to make Afghanistan a democracy with its own elected government *(1 mark KU)*. The operation was effective in the early days, successfully driving out al Qaeda but the Taliban has been much more resilient *(1 mark evaluative comment)*. **(Total 3 marks – 2 marks KU, 1 mark evaluation)** **Response 3** NATO has been involved in the Afghanistan war since 2001. This was an attempt to rid the country of al Qaeda and the Taliban after the attacks on 9/11. Over 150,000 NATO troops have served in Afghanistan, the bulk of these have been American soldiers. In 2010 the US had a 'surge' where it sent an extra 33,000 troops *(2 marks KU)*. ISAF has been successful in tackling al Qaeda. Afghanistan is no longer a 'safe haven' and Osama Bin Laden has been killed *(1 mark evaluation)*. However, the Afghanistan government has been weak and the Taliban have not been defeated. Most NATO troops pulled out in 2014 and many believe that it is only a matter of time until the Taliban re-emerge. NATOs success may well only be short term *(2 marks evaluation)*. **(Total 5 marks – 2 marks KU, 3 marks evaluation)** **Response 4** Over 3,000 NATO soldiers have been killed and there have been many civilian casualties too. While education and health systems have been created, the cost of the war in terms of casualties and finance has led some people to question how effective the intervention has been. **(Total 2 marks – 1 mark KU, 1 mark evaluation)**

HIGHER MODERN STUDIES
2017

Section 1 — Democracy in Scotland and the United Kingdom

Question	General Marking Instructions for this type of question	Max marks	Specific Marking Instructions for this question
1. (a)	Evaluation involves making judgments based on criteria, drawing conclusions on the extent to which a view is supported by the evidence; counter-arguments including possible alternative interpretations; the overall impact/significance of the factors when taken together; the relative importance of factors in relation to the context. Up to **8 marks** for KU (description, explanation and exemplification) and up to **4 marks** for analytical/evaluative comment. Award up to **6 marks** per point. Candidates should be credited up to **full marks** if they answer within a Scottish context only, a UK context only or refer to both Scotland and the UK.	12	*Candidates can be credited in a number of ways up to a maximum of 12 marks.* Credit reference to aspects of the following: **Single Transferable Vote** • A roughly proportionate voting system. Can be seen to deliver fair representation as percentage of votes cast for a party usually corresponds closely to the percentage of seats gained for a party. • STV more likely to result in coalition councils with more than one party in charge which means that more voters' views are heard and considered and, in theory, a wider range of policies introduced and implemented. • Voters rank candidates in order of preference and can choose from between and within political parties. The Electoral Reform Society maintain this can lead to better representation as elected representatives are more likely to be more responsive to needs of the voters. Can also make representatives more accountable. • Maintains a link between voter and representative which can be seen to deliver fairer representation. • Allows for by-elections should a representative die or resign whilst in post. **Balanced by** • STV often ends in coalitions which voters didn't directly vote for. • STV can often lead to parties with a small number of representatives holding the balance of power or becoming 'King Makers' which exaggerates and increases the power of the smaller parties. • STV is more likely to result in coalitions and these can be an unstable way of doing things as parties can fall out and coalitions disbanded. **First Past the Post** • FPTP is more likely to end with one party in charge which can be seen as being a more politically and economically stable form of government. • It allows the party that is the most popular with the voters the opportunity to carry out their manifesto commitments and promises without having to rely on the help of a 'junior partner' in government that could dilute and change the policies of government eg UK election 2015. • Maintains a direct link between voter and representative which can be seen to deliver fairer representation and increased accountability. • Allows for by elections should a representative die or resign whilst in post. **Balanced by** • Lack of proportionality means that it tends to favour the 'big two' (Cons/Lab) at the expense of smaller parties (Greens, Lib Dems etc). Now favours SNP in Scotland. • Government is often formed against the wishes of the majority of voters, eg, in 2015 the Conservatives won a Westminster majority with only 37% of the popular vote. Only 24% of voters eligible to vote actually voted for the Conservatives in 2015. • Can create two types of Parliamentary seats — safe and marginal which can often lead to disincentives for voters to vote for their preferred candidate or even tactical voting whereby voters vote to keep a candidate out as opposed to positively voting for a candidate.

Question	General Marking Instructions for this type of question	Max marks	Specific Marking Instructions for this question
1. (a)	(continued)		**AMS** • A roughly proportionate voting system. Can be seen to deliver fair representation as percentage of votes cast for a party usually corresponds closely to the percentage of seats gained for a party. • More likely that coalitions will be formed due to AMS which can be seen to be fairer as more opinions and points of view are likely to be heard and policies introduced that are more reflective of the wishes of the voters. • Allows smaller parties and single issue candidates greater opportunity of being elected and their voices heard in parliament (Greens, SSP, SSCUP, Dr Jean Turner etc). • List element of AMS gives greater opportunity for women and ethnic minority candidates to be elected if the parties select them. **Balanced by** • AMS often ends in coalitions which voters didn't directly vote for. • AMS can often lead to parties with a small number of representatives holding the balance of power or becoming 'King Makers' which exaggerates and increases the power of the smaller parties. Lib Dems in coalition government twice. • AMS is more likely to result in coalitions and these can be an unstable way of doing things as parties can fall out and coalitions disbanded. Although not happened in Scotland, evidence that it has occurred elsewhere. • With list part of AMS, there is no facility for by elections if candidate dies or resigns. The candidate who is next on the party's list gets to become the representative. • Gives great power to party leaders as they decide on candidates for lists. *Any other valid point that meets the criteria described in the general marking principles for this type of question.* **Possible approaches to answering this question:** **Response 1** Since STV was introduced for the first time in 2007, it can be argued that it provides for fair representation as it is likely that STV will lead to coalitions being formed. This can be seen to be fair as it results in more parties having a say in the running of local government in Scotland. For example, in 2007 only 2 of Scotland's 32 Councils were controlled by one party — Glasgow and North Lanarkshire. Indeed, 21 out of 32 councils had more than one party in charge. This shows that STV is better for representation as it is likely to lead to more voters' views being heard and policies introduced that will appeal to a wider range of voters. However, it could be argued that it does not lead to fair representation as councillors in a coalition may have to compromise and dilute their policies meaning that voters are not getting the promises they voted for. *(2 marks KU, 2 marks evaluation)* **Response 2** AMS is a proportionally representative voting system. It is used to elect MSPs to the Scottish Parliament with voters having two votes — One for a constituency MSP and the other vote elects representatives to a multi-member constituency. The result is roughly proportionate. This means that there will be fewer wasted votes as every vote in the List section counts and will reduce the need for tactical voting. The 2nd vote balances out the unfairness of the vote for the constituency MSP. For example, in 2011 the Conservatives only won 3 constituency seats but the 2nd vote meant their number of MSPs increased to 15 and made the number of MSPs they had more in line with the percentage of votes they received. *(2 marks KU, 2 marks evaluation)*

Question	General Marking Instructions for this type of question	Max marks	Specific Marking Instructions for this question
1. (a)	(continued)		**Response 3** First Past the Post is a plurality system used to elect UK MPs. It is a winner takes all system in which the candidate wins a parliamentary seat and gets to represent their constituency if they win more votes than the person in second. The party with the most seats gets to form the Government. Many people, and businesses, believe that FPTP is a fair system of voting as it is likely to lead to only one party being in charge which will mean more economic and political stability as the Government don't have to rely on the support of other parties. It also means that they can focus on carrying out their manifesto policies and run the country. This political and economic stability is good for our economy and jobs as companies are more likely to invest in countries that are stable and not in countries in which ruling parties are always falling out with each other. *(2 marks KU, 2 marks evaluation)*
(b)	Evaluation involves making judgments based on criteria, drawing conclusions on the extent to which a view is supported by the evidence; counter-arguments including possible alternative interpretations; the overall impact/ significance of the factors when taken together; the relative importance of factors in relation to the context. Up to **8 marks** for KU (description, explanation and exemplification) and up to **4 marks** for evaluative comments. Award up to **6 marks** per point. Candidates should be credited up to **full marks** if they answer within a Scottish context only, a UK context only or refer to both Scotland and the UK.	12	*Candidates can be credited in a number of ways **up to a maximum of 12 marks**.* Credit reference to aspects of the following: Scotland • FMQs • Work of Committees • Questions to Individual Ministers • Voting • Type of Government can affect effectiveness – Minority, Majority or Coalition • Size of Government Majority • Backbench Rebellion • Debates and Motions • Role and Power of the Whips • Decision Time UK • Prime Minister's Questions • Select Committees • Questions to Individual Ministers • Role of House of Lords as amending chamber • Power of the Whips • Type of Government – Minority, Majority and Coalition • Size of Government Majority • Backbench Rebellion • Early Day Motions/Ten Minute Bills • Voting • Salisbury Convention for policies in Government Manifesto Any other valid point that meets the criteria described in the general marking instructions for this kind of question. Possible approaches to answering this question: **Response 1** There are many ways in which Parliament can hold the Government to account. Parliamentary representatives like MPs can question the Prime Minister at PMQs every Wednesday. *(1 mark KU)* **Response 2** There are many ways in which parliament can hold the Government to account. Parliamentary representatives like MPs can question the Prime Minister at PMQs every Wednesday. PMQs is a good opportunity to hold the Government to account. PMQs can be effective as it has the potential to embarrass the PM, the Government and their policies. Jeremy Corbyn has asked many questions recently at PMQs particularly over the cuts to Tax Credits. However, many people think that PMQs are a wasted opportunity as many of the questions and PM responses are scripted and much of the time for holding to account is wasted on pre-prepared scripted responses. *(2 marks KU, 2 marks evaluation)*

Question	General Marking Instructions for this type of question	Max marks	Specific Marking Instructions for this question
1. (b)	(continued)		**Response 3** Parliament can be effective in holding the Scottish Government to account with the type of government in power being a big factor in deciding how effective parliament is. It is more difficult for parliament to hold to account if the government has the majority of MSPs. They can usually block any amendments and have more than enough MSPs to vote against any proposals put forward by other parties in the Parliament. If there is a majority government in power, then they can pass any difficult decisions like the budget quite easily. However, at the moment, there is a minority SNP government and they have to rely on the votes of other parties such as the Conservatives which make it easier for parliament to block or hold to account the work of government. The SNP has already compromised with Parliament in order to get things passed such as changes to the Council Tax. This shows that the type of government in power can often be a major factor in the effectiveness of parliament. *(3 marks KU, 2 marks evaluation)*
			Response 4 One of the main roles of parliament is to hold to account the work of government. Parliament can do this in many ways. They can ask questions of government ministers; they can take part in debates. They can also propose new laws themselves. Another good way is by proposing amendments to legislation put forward by the government. Parliament then votes on these amendments. In the UK, Parliament includes members of the House of Lords. Recently, the House of Lords voted against the Government during the cutting of Tax Credits debate. The House of Lords disagreed with the government and voted against the government's proposals. This embarrassed the government and has forced them to consider changing their plans. This shows that parliament has an important job and can hold to account the work of government. MPs also can be effective in holding to account the work of government such as forcing the government to seek changes to the 'Tampon Tax'. However, the success of MPs in Parliament is often dependent upon the type of government in power. A government with a small majority such as the 2015 Conservatives is more usually likely to be defeated and held to account by parliament more effectively than a government with a huge majority such as Tony Blair's majority of 166 in 1997. This highlights how parliament can be effective but is often sometimes limited by size and type of government. *(4 marks KU, 2 marks evaluation)*
2.	The candidate is required to interpret/evaluate up to three complex sources in order to reach conclusions. In order to achieve credit candidates must show evidence which explains the conclusions reached. • Award up to **3 marks** for appropriate use of evidence depending on the quality of the explanation and the synthesis of the evidence to reach any one conclusion. • For **full marks** candidates must refer to all sources in their answer.	8	*Candidates can be credited in a number of ways **up to a maximum of 8 marks**.* Possible approaches to answering the question: **The influence of poverty and social deprivation on voting behaviour.** **Response 1** One conclusion is that a person's level of wealth can influence how they vote. *(0 marks — valid conclusion but no evidence)* **Response 2** Source A suggests that the more wealthy a person is the more likely they are to vote No. This is backed up by source B which shows that those in social group ABC1 were more likely to vote No (57%) whereas those in C2DE were more likely to vote Yes (52%). This shows that a person's level of wealth influenced the way they voted with No voters having more wealth. *(2 marks, synthesis across sources A and B with conclusion)*

Question	General Marking Instructions for this type of question	Max marks	Specific Marking Instructions for this question
2.	(continued) • For **full marks** candidates must reach conclusions about each of the points given and make and overall conclusion on the issue.		**Response 3** Source A states that, the regions with higher levels of poverty were more likely to vote Yes. This is supported by source A and source C in areas such as Glasgow and Dundee with high levels of unemployment they were more likely to vote Yes. Moreover, in regions such as Aberdeen and East Renfrewshire they had low unemployment levels of 1.4% and also had large No majorities of 58% and 63%, which was the highest No majority in the table. This shows that there is a link between levels of poverty and deprivation and how people voted, ie lower poverty levels meant a lower Yes vote. *(3 marks for complex synthesis between all 3 sources and a conclusion. Having used all 3 sources correctly, the candidate can now access all 8 marks)* **The influence of age on voting behaviour.** **Response 4** Source B shows that nearly three quarters of voters aged 65 plus voted No. However, there were more Yes voters in the age brackets 16–24, 25–34, 35–44 and 45–54 but the margin was much narrower. This shows that age was a factor particularly within older voters and encouraged them to vote "No" *(2 marks for synthesis of information within source B)* **Possible overall conclusion about the most important factors influencing the outcome of the Scottish Independence Referendum** **Response 6** The overall conclusion is that poverty levels were the most significant in influencing the outcome. Those regions that voted Yes – Glasgow, Dundee, North Lanarkshire and West Dunbartonshire had the highest levels of child poverty. *(2 marks for valid conclusion with evidence from sources A + C)* **Response 7** Although several factors were important in deciding the outcome, such as age, deprivation etc, these are all less important than gender. Women voted decisively for the "No" side. This 58% No vote swung the result that way. The male "No" vote was only 53%. It is clear that the No majority among women was vital in creating the No decision. *(2 marks – valid conclusion, evidence and evaluative comment)* **Response 8** Social class was important in deciding the result. *(0 marks – valid conclusion, no evidence)* **Please note that a valid conclusion which is not supported with relevant source evidence should be given no credit.** *Any other valid point that meets the criteria described in the general marking principles for this kind of question.*

Section 2 — Social Issues in the United Kingdom

Question	General Marking Instructions for this type of question	Max marks	Specific Marking Instructions for this question
3. (a)	An analysis mark should be awarded where a candidate uses their knowledge and understanding/a source, to identify relevant components (eg of an idea, theory, argument, etc) and clearly show at least one of the following: • links between different components • links between component(s) and the whole • links between components(s) and related concepts • similarities and contradictions • consistency and inconsistency • different views/interpretations • possible consequences/implications • the relative importance of components • understanding of underlying order or structure Evaluation involves making a judgments based on criteria, drawing conclusions on the extent to which a view is supported by the evidence; counter-arguments including possible alternative interpretations; the overall impact/significance of the factors when taken together; the relative importance of factors in relation to the context. Credit responses that: • make reference to health inequalities across the UK and how poverty can cause poor health • provide balanced evaluative comments referring to different causes of poor health and their relative importance • provide a clear, coherent line of argument. Up to **8 marks** for KU (description, explanation and exemplification) and up to **12 marks** for analytical/evaluative comments. Award up to **6 marks** per point. Candidates should be credited up to full marks if they answer within a Scottish context only, a UK context only or refer to both Scotland and the UK as appropriate Where a candidate makes more analytical/evaluative points than are required to gain the maximum allocation of **4 marks**, these can be credited as knowledge and understanding marks provided they meet the criteria for this.	20	*Candidates can be credited in a number of ways up to a maximum of 20 marks.* **Credit reference to aspects of the following:** • Health reports including Equally Well (2008 & 2010), Audit Scotland (2012). • Evidence of health inequalities and their link to poverty rates. • Impact of poverty on health: welfare dependency, poor housing, effect on mental health. • Harry Burn's research on 'biology of poverty' and impact of chaotic childhood. 'Sense of coherence' triangle and impact of poverty on ability to develop resilience, longer recovery from illnesses in deprived areas of Glasgow. • The 'Glasgow effect' — Glasgow has the lowest life expectancy in Europe, research by the Glasgow Centre for Population and Health shows that health outcomes in Glasgow are worse than those in cities facing similar poverty levels such as Liverpool and Manchester. • Other factors: lifestyle choice (smoking, alcohol, diet, exercise), hereditary factors, gender, race, access to medical care. *Any other valid point that meets the criteria described in the general marking instructions for this kind of question.* **Possible approaches to answering this question:** **Response 1** Within the UK there remains a health inequality between the least deprived and the most deprived communities. Life expectancy in the least deprived communities remains much higher than in the most deprived communities with women in the least deprived living until 84 compared to 76 for those in the most deprived and men living to 81 in the least deprived and 70 in the most deprived. This shows that there is a continuing trend where people in the poorest communities face health inequalities and poverty can be argued to be linked to poor health. *(1 mark KU, 1 mark analysis)* **Response 2** Children growing up in a deprived community can experience health inequalities due to environmental factors that affect their health. The Poverty and Social Exclusion survey of 2013 found that 18 million people in the UK cannot afford adequate housing conditions and that 2.5 million children live in homes that are damp. This can lead to health issues such as asthma and eczema which can impact on a child's immune system. Furthermore, Dr Harry Burns concluded in the Equally Well report that difficult social circumstances in the early years can have an effect on the body's host defences. He argued that the chronic stress experienced by those living in poverty can make health inequalities worse and increase the risk of an individual dying from the big killer diseases. Therefore, poverty contributes significantly to an individual's health and therefore is the main cause of health inequalities. *(3 marks KU, 1 mark analysis, 1 mark evaluation)* **Response 3** Lifestyle factors such as poor diet, and a lack of exercise can also impact on a person's health. A lack of exercise and a poor diet can lead to an individual being obese and develop high blood pressure, coronary heart disease and type 2 diabetes. Across Scotland only 55% of 13–15 year olds complete 60 minutes of physical activity a day which shows that lifestyle choices are also impacting on health and that poverty is not the only cause of poor health. *(1 mark KU, 1 mark analysis, 1 mark evaluation)*

Question		General Marking Instructions for this type of question	Max marks	Specific Marking Instructions for this question
3.	(b)	An analysis mark should be awarded where a candidate uses their knowledge and understanding/a source, to identify relevant components (eg of an idea, theory, argument, etc) and clearly show at least one of the following: • links between different components • links between component(s) and the whole • links between component(s) and related concepts • similarities and contradictions • consistency and inconsistency • different views/interpretations • possible consequences/implications • the relative importance of components • understanding of underlying order or structure Evaluation involves making a judgments based on criteria, drawing conclusions on the extent to which a view is supported by the evidence; counter-arguments including possible alternative interpretations; the overall impact/significance of the factors when taken together; the relative importance of factors in relation to the context. Credit responses that: • make reference to government policies that have targeted social and economic inequalities • provide a balanced overall evaluative comment on the effectiveness of government policies in reducing social and economic inequalities Up to **8 marks** for KU (description, explanation and exemplification) and up to **12 marks** for analytical/evaluative comments. Award up to **6 marks** per point. Candidates should be credited up to **full marks** if they answer within a Scottish context only, a UK context only or refer to both Scotland and the UK as appropriate Where a candidate makes more analytical/evaluative points than are required to gain the **maximum allocation of 4 marks**, these can be credited as knowledge and understanding marks provided they meet the criteria for this.	20	*Candidates can be credited in a number of ways **up to a maximum of 20 marks**.* **Credit reference to aspects of the following:** • The benefits system — Universal Credit, Tax Credits, Jobseekers Allowance, Child Benefit, State Pensions. • National Minimum Wage and the Living Wage campaign. • The impact of austerity measures and government cuts to welfare. • The Equality Act 2010 and reference to Equality and Human Rights Commission reports. • The NHS and policies to reduce health inequality; the smoking ban 2006; free prescription charges, recommendations of Equally Well Report. *Any other valid point that meets the criteria described in the general marking instructions for this kind of question.* **Possible approaches to answering this question:** **Response 1** One policy introduced to tackle inequalities in wealth is the National Minimum Wage which was introduced in 1999 as a way of tackling poverty amongst low paid workers. At the time it was effective in reducing economic inequalities as it raised the pay of 1.3 million workers. Furthermore, according to the Low Pay Commission, 2 million workers have benefited from recent increases in the NMW, significantly ¾ of these are women. This shows that people are earning more and that government attempts to tackle wealth inequality through the NMW have been partly effective in reducing low income. However, it is now argued that the NMW is not sufficient to meet minimum living standards, according to research by the Joseph Rowntree Foundation, in 2015 single people need to earn at least £17,000 to achieve a minimum income standard, while couples with two children need to earn at least £20,000 each. A full time minimum wage job at £6.70 an hour will lead to an annual wage of around £12,000 which is significantly below the requirements of a minimum income standard, showing that government policies have not managed to effectively reduce economic inequalities experienced by those working at a minimum wage. *(2 marks KU, 2 marks analysis, 2 marks evaluation)* **Response 2** The UK Government has recently reformed the benefit system and introduced the Universal Credit which brings together into one payment previous benefits and tax credits such as Job-Seekers Allowance, Employment and Support Allowance and Working Tax Credits. This was introduced to reduce the number of people trapped in benefits by increasing the amount people in low paid work can claim. The government think that 3.1 million households will be entitled to claim more, in particular working couples with children will benefit. *(2 marks KU, 1 mark analysis)* **Response 3** The UK Government has tried to reduce social inequalities by introducing the Equality Act of 2010. This gives greater powers to people facing discrimination for a 'protected characteristic' and so helps to reduce inequalities in employment and social life. For example, there remains a gender pay gap in the UK, and the Equality Act gives greater powers to women to sue their employer for discrimination in pay. *(2 marks KU)*

Question		General Marking Instructions for this type of question	Max marks	Specific Marking Instructions for this question
3.	(c)	An analysis mark should be awarded where a candidate uses their knowledge and understanding/a source, to identify relevant components (eg of an idea, theory, argument, etc) and clearly show at least one of the following: • links between different components • links between component(s) and the whole • links between component(s) and related concepts • similarities and contradictions • consistency and inconsistency • different views/interpretations • possible consequences/implications • the relative importance of components • understanding of underlying order or structure Evaluation involves making judgments based on criteria, drawing conclusions on the extent to which a view is supported by the evidence; counter-arguments including possible alternative interpretations; the overall impact/significance of the factors when taken together; the relative importance of factors in relation to the context. Credit responses that: • make reference to individual choice as a cause of crime • provide balanced evaluative comments referring to different factors and their relative importance • Provide a clear, coherent line of argument. Up to **8 marks** for KU (description, explanation and exemplification) and up to **12 marks** for analytical/evaluative comments. Award up to **6 marks** per point. Candidates should be credited up to full marks if they answer within a Scottish context only, a UK context only or refer to both Scotland and the UK as appropriate Where a candidate makes more analytical/evaluative points than are required to gain the maximum allocation of **4 marks**, these can be credited as knowledge and understanding marks provided they meet the criteria for this.	20	*Candidates can be credited in a number of ways up to a maximum of 20 marks.* **Credit reference to aspects of the following:** • Theories of crime such as individualistic — free will, psychological causes; sociological-functionalism, control theory, labelling; and biological causes of crime. • Family background. • Lack of education. • Poverty and social exclusion. • Peer pressure. • Drugs and alcohol. *Any other valid point that meets the criteria described in the general marking instructions for this kind of question.* **Possible approaches to answering this question:** **Response 1** Some people may be more likely to commit crime because of a lack of success in education. This could lead to higher unemployment and therefore people may resort to crime such as theft instead. *(1 mark KU)* **Response 2** Family relationships can lead people to commit more crime. Children brought up in a deprived childhood and also where they have experienced poor parenting can be more likely to be involved in crime as they become older. John Bowlby's attachment theory argues that children who do not have a strong emotional attachment to a parent can become more anxious and suffer from low self-esteem and negative self-image. This means that if parents themselves are involved in criminal behaviour than their children will learn this behaviour through socialisation and go on to commit crime themselves. Therefore, poor parenting can be a very influential cause of crime as it can inform adult behaviour on a long-term basis and impact on how a person responds to later adverse conditions. *(2 marks KU, 1 mark analysis, 1 mark evaluation)* **Response 3** One factor that can cause crime is poverty. In areas of high unemployment and social exclusion you are more likely to have higher crime rates. There is a clear link between poverty and certain types of crime. For example, Glasgow has the highest level of poverty with 6 of the 10 poorest constituencies in the UK being in the city. It has also some of the highest levels of crime such as theft, housebreaking and assault. This shows that there is a clear link between poverty deprivation and crime. Theorists like Robert Merton argued that as a result of delinquent sub-cultures that can develop in areas like these, people commit crime in order to obtain things they can't afford and to reach society's goals. However, Merton's ideas have been criticised as they do not always explain why some people who live in extreme poverty never consider committing a crime. Clearly there is an element of individual choice as to why some people commit crime. *(3 marks KU, 2 marks analysis, 1 mark evaluation)*

Question		General Marking Instructions for this type of question	Max marks	Specific Marking Instructions for this question
3.	**(d)**	An analysis mark should be awarded where a candidate uses their knowledge and understanding/a source, to identify relevant components (eg of an idea, theory, argument, etc) and clearly show at least one of the following: • links between different components • links between component(s) and the whole • links between component(s) and related concepts • similarities and contradictions • consistency and inconsistency • different views/interpretations • possible consequences/implications • the relative importance of components • understanding of underlying order or structure Evaluation involves making judgments based on criteria, drawing conclusions on the extent to which a view is supported by the evidence; counter-arguments including possible alternative interpretations; the overall impact/significance of the factors when taken together; the relative importance of factors in relation to the context. Credit responses that: • make reference to the prison system in Scotland and/or the UK • provide balance evaluative comments referring to the effectiveness of prisons in tackling crime • provide a clear, coherent line of argument Up to **8 marks** for KU (description, explanation and exemplification) and up to **12 marks** for analytical/ evaluative comments. Award up to **6 marks** per point. Candidates should be credited up to **full marks** if they answer within a Scottish context only, a UK context only or refer to both Scotland and the UK as appropriate Where a candidate makes more analytical/evaluative points than are required to gain the maximum allocation of **4 marks**, these can be credited as knowledge and understanding marks provided they meet the criteria for this.	20	*Candidates can be credited in a number of ways **up to a maximum of 20 marks.*** **Credit reference to aspects of the following:** • Aims of the prison service — to protect the public by maintaining secure custody, humane care for offenders, reduce reoffending, value for money. • Prison as a deterrence and punishment. • Reoffending rates for different lengths of sentence and recommendations of Audit Scotland 2012 report. • Ability of a prison sentence to address crimes linked to drug and alcohol addictions. • Criminal Justice and Licensing Act 2010 to reduce prison sentences less than 3 months. • Alternatives to prison — Community Payback orders, Restorative Justice. • 2012 Commission on Women Offenders report and criticism of Cornton Vale. References can be made to Scottish and/or UK prisons *Any other valid point that meets the criteria described in the general marking instructions for this kind of question.* **Possible approaches to answering this question:** **Response 1** One aim of prison is to act as a deterrent to crime as it takes away the human right of freedom. As such many people will not commit a crime for fear of receiving a prison sentence. *(1 mark KU)* **Response 2** One aim of a prison sentence is to protect the public by keeping dangerous offenders in custody. This can tackle crime as it means that violent offenders such as Dale Cregan who killed 4 people, including 2 police officers in 2012. Dale Cregan is currently serving a whole life sentence as the murder of PC Bone and PC Hughes was considered by the courts to be cold blooded and premeditated. This shows that prisons can effectively meet their aim of protecting the public by keeping the most violent offenders in prison for their whole life and therefore prevent them from committing further crime. *(2 marks KU, 1 mark evaluation)* **Response 3** Prisons aim to reduce reoffending rates by providing rehabilitation programmes and education for those serving a prison sentence. However, reoffending rates across the UK remain very high with 46% of adults in England and Wales reconvicted within a year of release, this is particularly high for those serving sentences of less than one year. Where prisons have focused on education to help rehabilitate offenders they have been more effective at reducing reoffending. Prisoners with access to education had a reoffending rate of 19% compared to 26% for similar inmates without education. Providing educational opportunities for those in prison can help them gain employment when they are released and stop them falling back into a life of crime when released. This shows that prisons remain ineffective in reoffending rates and therefore tackling crime, particularly amongst offenders committing crimes that lead to a prison sentence less than a year. *(2 marks KU, 2 marks analysis, 2 marks evaluation)*

Section 3 — International Issues

Question	General Marking Instructions for this type of question	Max marks	Specific Marking Instructions for this question
4. (a)	An analysis mark should be awarded where a candidate uses their knowledge and understanding/a source, to identify relevant components (eg of an idea, theory, argument, etc) and clearly show at least one of the following: • links between different components • links between component(s) and the whole • links between component(s) and related concepts • similarities and contradictions • consistency and inconsistency • different views/interpretations • possible consequences/implications • the relative importance of components • understanding of underlying order or structure Up to **8 marks** for KU (description, explanation and exemplification) and up to **4 marks** for analytical comments Award up to **6 marks** per point. Where a candidate makes more evaluative points than are required to gain the maximum allocation of **4 marks**, these can be credited as knowledge and understanding marks provided they meet the criteria for this.	12	**Credit responses that make reference to:** • Areas where people are affected by a socio economic issue. • An analysis of ways in which people are affected by a socio economic issue. **Possible approaches to answering the question:** **World Power: USA** **Credit reference to aspects of the following:** • Reference may be made to income/wealth/poverty levels, employment/unemployment rates, housing, education, health and healthcare and crime. • African Americans/Hispanics still groups least likely to have health insurance despite Obamacare 50% of African Americans and 42% of Hispanics compared to 74% of Whites. Although an additional 9.5 million aged 16—64 had obtained health insurance since Obamacare was launched. • Health related illnesses evident within and between groups/individuals. 50% of African Americans are obese and report lower life expectancy. • African Americans/Hispanics still report lower household incomes compared to Whites and Asian Americans. • African Americans remain almost 3 times as likely to be living in poverty compared to Whites. • A 'funding gap' is evident in schools in deprived areas mostly attended by ethnic minorities leading to inequalities in educational attainment. • Higher drop-out rates for African Americans and Hispanics compared to Asian Americans who make up 10% of undergraduates yet only 5% of population. • Home ownership rates vary across groups; in 2014 72% of whites owned their own home, in comparison to around 45% of Hispanics and 43% of African Americans. • However, since economic recession in 2008, all ethnic groups have faced difficulties with home ownership with an estimated 11 million homes being repossessed. • Growing middle class amongst African Americans who report higher salaries and have been able to 'lift' themselves out of poverty and move to better neighbourhoods which have better access to education and employment opportunities such as Atlanta and Los Angeles. *Any other valid point that meets the criteria described in the general marking instructions for this kind of question.* **World Power: South Africa** • Reference may be made to income/wealth/poverty levels, employment/unemployment rates, housing, education, health and healthcare and crime. • Almost half of South Africans are living below the poverty line, surviving on just over R500 a month. • Widening gap between rich and poor with lowest 5% of population getting little of the top 10% share of income — Estimated 450,000 whites, of a total white population of 4.5 million, live below the poverty line. • 12.8 million (86,4%) households had access to piped water in 2013 compared to 9.4 million (79,9%) in 2005 however there is variation between households regarding the standard of service and quality of water. • In 2011, two-thirds of those who had no education were living in poverty. • The unemployment rate of 15—24 year olds with primary education or less is 50%; for those with tertiary level education, the unemployment rate is 37%.

Question		General Marking Instructions for this type of question	Max marks	Specific Marking Instructions for this question
4.	(a)	(continued)		• 1.3 million blacks (14% of the black workforce) earn as much as or more than the average white. In 2000, the average black South African earned 15% of the average white South African's income, whereas in 2011, an average black person earned 40% of an average white person's income. • The official unemployment rate for black South Africans in 2012 was 29.1% compared to 23.9% for coloureds, 9.3% for Indian/Asians and 6.1% for whites. • Only 41% of adults are employed. • Creation of black middle class (the 'Cappuccino Society') and black elite ('Black Diamonds'). • 5.8 million blacks own their own property. • The average white person's income is currently rising by 5.3% a year, whereas the average black person's income is rising by 14.9%. • Increase of poverty amongst whites. • Based on the national definition of poverty — $4 a day- more than half of South Africans (54%) are poor and poverty and inequality still reflect race. *Any other valid point that meets the criteria described in the general marking instructions for this kind of question.* **Possible approaches to answering the question** **World Power: USA** **Response 1** Many individuals experience economic inequalities through income. Certain groups in the USA have a higher household income than others. In 2012, African American and Hispanics had lower household incomes than white and Asian Americans. On average, Asian Americans earned more than twice as much as African Americans. *(2 marks KU)* **Response 2** Many individuals experience economic inequalities through income. Certain groups in the USA have a higher household income than others. In 2012, African American and Hispanics had lower household incomes than White and Asian Americans. On average, Asian Americans earned more than twice as much as African Americans. Those who have a lower income are more likely to be in poverty. African Americans are almost three times as likely to be living in poverty compared to whites although there has been progress made with a growing black middle class who have lifted themselves out of poverty and moved to better areas such as Atlanta and Los Angeles which now have thriving middle class communities. *(3 marks KU, 2 marks analysis)* **Response 3** Many Americans experience inequalities in education as a result of schools in more affluent areas gaining more funding than schools in poorer areas. This often impacts on African Americans and Hispanics more than whites and Asian Americans as these two ethnic groups tend to live in areas where schools are of a lower standard. The 'funding gap' is illustrated by school graduation rates. In 2013 83% of Whites graduated in comparison to 71% of Hispanics and 66% of African Americans. However, not all ethnic groups experience inequalities in education, Asian Americans report low high school drop-out rates and make up 10% of undergraduates despite only making up 5% of the total US population. For many individuals the inequalities they face in educational attainment can lead to further inequalities in employment and health in later life. *(2 marks KU, 4 marks analysis)*

Question		General Marking Instructions for this type of question	Max marks	Specific Marking Instructions for this question
4.	(a)	(continued)		**Response 4** As the USA does not have a national health service, Americans rely on private health insurance to provide medical cover. Many Americans do not have health insurance due to the barrier of cost. Ethnic minorities are more likely to be uninsured therefore receive poor quality care, suffer more health problems and die prematurely. This is reflected in the fact 50% of African Americans, 42% of Hispanics have private health insurance compared to 74% of whites. However, since the introduction of Obama's Affordable Care Act in 2010 an additional 9.5 million people aged 19–64 have obtained health insurance. Although some have argued that the act has focused more on making sure people are covered than it does on addressing the cost of care in the first place. Despite the rise in the number of Americans with health insurance in recent years, 50% of African Americans are obese and the life expectancy of ethnic minorities remains low compared to other groups. *(4 marks KU, 4 marks analysis – this candidate has covered two distinct points in relation to the issue.)*
	(b)	An analysis mark should be awarded where a candidate uses their knowledge and understanding/a source, to identify relevant components (eg of an idea, theory, argument, etc.) and clearly show at least one of the following: • links between different components • links between component(s) and the whole • links between component(s) and related concepts • similarities and contradictions • consistency and inconsistency • different views/interpretations • possible consequences/implications • the relative importance of components • understanding of underlying order or structure Up to **8 marks** for KU (description, explanation and exemplification) and up to **4 marks** for analytical comments Award up to **6 marks** per point. Where a candidate makes more evaluative points than are required to gain the maximum allocation of **4 marks**, these can be credited as knowledge and understanding marks provided they meet the criteria for this.	12	**Credit responses that make reference to:** • Description of political opportunities for people to participate. • An analysis of how different political opportunities can influence decision making. **Possible approaches to answering the question:** **World Power: China** **Credit reference to aspects of the following:** • Voting in elections at various levels. • Membership of political parties. • Standing as a candidate in elections. • Party activism. • Interest group membership. • Activity protest/direct action. • Citizens can apply to become members of the Communist Party but only a small percentage is actually invited to join. In 2011 over 22 million applied but only 3 million were accepted. Membership brings high status and privilege. • Citizens can only vote at local level. Only candidates and parties sanctioned by the Communist Party are allowed to seek election. Eight other parties are legal but do not act as "opposition" eg China Democratic League, Chinese Peasants' and Workers' Democratic Party. The Democratic League has over 200,000 members. • Some pressure group activity is allowed but it cannot question the authority or legitimacy of the Communist Party. Many dissidents have been in prison since Tiananmen Square and others have been exiled eg Wei Jingshen. • Some protests are now tolerated provided they are not pro-democracy eg Environmental groups have grown in number eg many campaigned against the building of the Three Gorges Dam. These groups have experienced limited success and have become popular. • All China's Women's Federation provides women with the opportunity to campaign on issues such as women's rights. • All-China Federation of Trade Unions although trade unions are not independent organisations, they have increasingly allowed members the opportunity to campaign on issues relating to workers' rights. *Any other valid point that meets the criteria described in the general marking instructions for this kind of question.*

uestion		General Marking Instructions for this type of question	Max marks	Specific Marking Instructions for this question
4.	(b)	(continued)		**World Power: USA** **Credit reference to aspects of the following:**

World Power: USA

Credit reference to aspects of the following:

- Membership of an interest group eg the NRA to campaign against proposed firearm legislation. The NRA has proved successful at State level in loosening gun laws gaining 230 full legislative victories over the last 10 years. Most recently, as a result of the Sandy Hook School massacre, there was a relaxing of gun restrictions to allow armed volunteers to guard schools.
- Use of media; social networking to publicise and fundraise campaigns.
- Petitions to lobby representatives at local, state and federal level. In 2011 the White House created a petitioning website called "We the People". Petitions that gather 25,000 or more signatures within 30 days receive an administration response.
- Membership of a political party eg Democrats or Republicans.
- Voting and standing as a candidate at local, state or federal level. A single voter may be able to vote for up to 30 officials and representatives at one election.

Any other valid point that meets the criteria described in the general marking instructions for this kind of question.

Possible approaches to answering the question

World Power: China

Response 1
There are some opportunities for people to participate politically in China such as voting in village elections. Elections are held every three years and any villager who is aged 18 or above can vote. At these elections people also have the opportunity to put themselves forward as a candidate for election. *(2 marks KU)*

Response 2
There are some opportunities for people to participate politically in China such as voting in village elections. Elections are held every three years and any villager who is aged 18 or above can vote. At these elections people also have the opportunity to put themselves forward as a candidate for election however candidates are often selected in a process that some say is not always open and transparent. Village committees are limited to decisions on land reform. Decisions regarding more serious issues are made at national or provincial level. *(2 marks KU, 2 marks analysis)*

Response 3
Many citizens have exercised their political right to protest against Communist Party rule in China. Chinese people can take part in protests and demonstrations however only if they are approved by the CPC therefore limiting their influence on decision making. Some protests are now tolerated such as single issue protests eg demand to be connected to the country's high speed rail network however protests for democracy are forbidden and are often met with military force. In March 2011 a number of Chinese people gathered in pro-democracy protests across 13 cities and in 2014 large scale protests took place in Hong Kong, as tens of thousands of people set up camps in a protest that lasted two months. Dissidents were arrested, reports of mistreatment are not uncommon however little progress has been made showing decision making is limited. *(3 marks KU, 3 marks analysis)*

Question		General Marking Instructions for this type of question	Max marks	Specific Marking Instructions for this question
4.	(c)	An analysis mark should be awarded where a candidate uses their knowledge and understanding/a source, to identify relevant components (eg of an idea, theory, argument, etc) and clearly show at least one of the following: • links between different components • links between component(s) and the whole • links between component(s) and related concepts • similarities and contradictions • consistency and inconsistency • different views/interpretations • possible consequences/implications • the relative importance of components • understanding of underlying order or structure Up to **8 marks** for KU (description, explanation and exemplification) and up to **4 marks** for analytical comments Award up to **6 marks** per point. Where a candidate makes more evaluative points than are required to gain the maximum allocation of **4 marks**, these can be credited as knowledge and understanding marks provided they meet the criteria for this.	12	**Credit responses that make reference to:** • Background of world issue. • Analysis of the difficulties faced in resolving the issue. **Depending on the world issue chosen, candidates may make reference to any relevant factors, such as:** • Individual countries. • International organisations. **Possible approaches to answering the question:** **World Issue: Terrorism** • Lack of intelligence on planned/suspected attacks. • Rise of ISIS; Increase of random, smaller attacks. Recruitment of Jihads. • Range of tactics used by individuals and terrorist organisations to carry out attacks. • Increase of home-grown terrorist groups linked to al-Qaed eg in Somalia and Nigeria who take advantage of lack of infrastructure and policing to recruit and train people. • Increase in radicalisation. • 'Home grown' terrorists. **World Issue: Conflict eg Middle East, Ukraine, Syria, Iraq, Afghanistan** • Poor governance to deliver key services. • Kleptocracy — funds diverted to equip the military. • Cost of armed conflict. • Displacement of people from their homes destroying prospects of becoming self-sufficient. • International Organisations often restricted in accessing certain countries. • Lack of funding for international organisations to provide aid/supplies. **World Issue: Poverty in the developing world** • Lack of education. • Lack of infrastructure — impact on trade. • Lack of universal health care to educate in prevention and treatment eg HIV/AIDs, outbreak of illnesses eg Ebola. • Lack of adequate sanitation facilities. • High levels of debt. • Poor governance and corruption. • Lack of funding for international organisations to provide aid/supplies. **Possible approaches to answering the question** **World Issue: Terrorism** **Response 1** The growth of random attacks carried out by terrorists has created challenges in ensuring there are enough resources to respond to the threat of attacks. In light of the Charlie Hebdo attacks in Paris and the beach attacks in Tunisia, increased security patrols have been put in place as a precautionary measure against the threat of another attack. Such measures are designed to protect and reassure the public. *(2 marks KU)*

Question		General Marking Instructions for this type of question	Max marks	Specific Marking Instructions for this question
4.	(c)	(continued)		**Response 2** The growth of random attacks carried out by terrorists has created challenges in ensuring there are enough resources to respond to the threat of attacks. In light of the Charlie Hedbo attacks in Paris and the beach attacks in Tunisia, increased security patrols have been put in place as a precautionary measure against the threat of another attack. Such measures are designed to protect and reassure the public. However, increasing the number of security officers would require additional funding in order to be able to respond effectively. The current counter terrorism budget for protecting the UK public is only £130 million a year which would make it difficult for security forces to be expected to stop every plot. *(2 marks KU, 2 marks analysis)* **Response 3** The UK terror alert remains at severe, meaning a terrorist attack is highly likely. At least 700 people from the UK are believed to have travelled to support or fight for Jihadist organisations in Syria and Iraq. Many of those who have travelled are women and children who have been recruited online and hid their plans from their families. The increased number of Britons being radicalised through the internet is unclear but the use of social networking and propaganda videos has a role to play in persuading young people to follow, which has made it very difficult for authorities to detect. Since nearly half of those who have travelled to Syria for Jihadist causes were previously unknown to authorities it has added pressure for intelligence services to intercept communications to be vigilant. *(2 marks KU, 2 marks analysis)* **Response 4** The UK terror alert remains at severe, meaning a terrorist attack is highly likely. At least 700 people from the UK are believed to have travelled to support or fight for Jihadist organisations in Syria and Iraq. Many of those who have travelled are women and children who have been recruited online and hid their plans from their families. The increased number of Britons being radicalised through the internet is unclear but the use of social networking and propaganda videos has a role to play in persuading young people to follow. Since nearly half of those who have travelled to Syria for Jihadist causes were previously unknown to authorities it has added pressure for intelligence services to intercept communications to be vigilant. Head of MI5 recently stated the shape of the terror threat has changed due to the way terrorists use secure and encrypted apps to broadcast their message and incite terrorism. Many claim the existing legislation for surveillance online does not go far enough however, increasing the volume of monitoring raises ethical concerns over invasion of privacy. *(3 marks KU, 3 marks analysis)*

Question	General Marking Instructions for this type of question	Max marks	Specific Marking Instructions for this question
4. (d)	An analysis mark should be awarded where a candidate uses their knowledge and understanding/a source, to identify relevant components (eg of an idea, theory, argument, etc) and clearly show at least one of the following: • links between different components • links between component(s) and the whole • links between components(s) and related concepts • similarities and contradictions • consistency and inconsistency • different views/interpretations • possible consequences/implications • the relative importance of components • understanding of underling order or structure Up to **8 marks** for KU (description, explanation and exemplification) and up to **4 marks** for analytical comments Award up to **6 marks** per point Award up to **6 marks** per point. Where a candidate makes more evaluative points than are required to gain the maximum allocation of **4 marks**, these can be credited as knowledge and understanding marks provided they meet the criteria for this	12	**Credit responses that make reference to:** • Background of world issue. • The effects of the world issue. **Possible approaches to answering the question:** **World Issue: Terrorism** • Pressure on some governments to "do more" to protect people. Pressure from sympathetic political factions in own country eg Nigeria. • Businesses trading on global market can experience short term effects following an attack — economic difficulties for countries. • Armed forces of countries deployed to stabilise and support countries affected by terrorism. Defence forces on active duty fighting terrorist forces eg Taliban, ISIS, Al-Qaeda — Financial/human/infrastructure costs. • Governments of individual countries in planning and managing security for large scale and major events. Increased expense for security in public places eg UK state opening of parliament, U.S Presidential inauguration. • Tourism for businesses/countries in light of political unrest eg Egypt, Tunisia. • Unemployment, poverty, dependency on aid. **World Issue: Conflict** • Children suffer from armed conflict. Children often become orphans or are recruited as child soldiers — damages economy, long term social/economic problems for the country in the future. • Large numbers of citizens are often displaced from their homes and forced to live in refugee camps. Normal activity impossible, causes increased costs to the government to manage disease/welfare etc. • Vast numbers of refugees are left without food, water, shelter and medical support. Causes increased pressure on infrastructure and massive re-build costs eg Aleppo. • Land owners often face their crops being destroyed which affects food production which would impact on health of population/cause famine **World Issue: poverty in the developing world** • Children are group most likely to be malnourished; poor nutrition plays a role in around half of all child deaths in Africa, little prospect of economic development plus costs, health, etc impacting on future development of country. • Lack of educated workforce; high rates of adult illiteracy leading to low paid jobs/unemployment, again economic underdevelopment, low government revenue impacts on future development of country. • Farmers invested in cash crops that depend heavily on exporting crops, proportion of land being leased to foreign companies to grow their own cash crops creating dependency for many families. Over-reliance of country on foreign companies/governments/aid. • Malnourished families — can contribute to low life expectancy, infant deaths, long term effects on ability to work and loss of earnings. High costs/low productivity can impact on country. • Girls who cannot afford to attend school — An estimated 31 million girls of primary school age and 32 million girls of lower secondary school age were out of school in 2013. Education can help break the cycle of poverty but it is a long term investment that the countries/governments cannot afford.

uestion	General Marking Instructions for this type of question	Max marks	Specific Marking Instructions for this question
4. (d)	(continued)		**Possible approaches to answering the question** **World Issue: Conflict** **Response 1** Children suffer seriously from armed conflict. In Syria an increasing number of children are recruited by armed groups to fight for the conflict. Children are often used as informers, porters, guards and in some cases fighters. After the conflict many children are traumatised and unable to contribute to the country. *(2 marks KU)* **Response 2** Children suffer seriously from armed conflict. In Syria an increasing number of children are recruited by armed groups to fight for the conflict. Children are often used as informers, porters, guards and in some cases fighters. This can impact on them psychologically and physically as many are expelled from their community leading to the community not having a sufficient workforce. *(2 marks KU, 1 mark analysis)* **Response 3** Children can often become orphans as their parents are caught up in the conflict. In the last decade more than 1 million children have been orphaned or separated from their parents as a result many often find themselves uprooted from their homes which impacts on their education. Almost 50 million primary and lower secondary aged pupils are out of school in conflict affected areas. Due to missing large periods of education due to fighting or displacement, the country's future prospects and ability to become self-sufficient are limited. A further impact is that girls who are out of school are more vulnerable to sexual violence and early pregnancy. This causes a cost to the health service within the country and can also contribute to a breakdown within communities and social breakdown in the country. *(3 marks KU, 3 marks analysis)*
5.	The candidate is required to interpret/evaluate up to three complex sources of information detecting and explaining the extent of objectivity. In order to achieve credit candidates must show evidence which supports the extent of accuracy in a given viewpoint. • Award up to **3 marks** for appropriate use of evidence depending on the quality of the explanation and the synthesis of the evidence for any one explanation of the extent of objectivity. • For **full marks** candidates must refer to all sources in their answer. • For **full marks** candidates must make an overall judgment as to the extent of the accuracy of the given statement. • Maximum of **6 marks** if no overall judgement made on extent of accuracy of the statement.	8	Candidates can be credited in a number of ways **up to a maximum of 8 marks**. **Evidence that supports the view ("women now have greater political influence")** **Examples of the types of evidence that support the view include:** • Source A, first female elected councillors. • Source A, 4–17 women elected. • Source A, first woman beat seven men in vote. • Sources B + C, 30 women appointed to the Shura Council. • Source B + C, women allowed to vote in local council elections, 130,000 registered. • Source B – 978 female candidates. **Response 1** Women clearly do experience greater influence in politics as they are now allowed to take part in elections and have elected the first 17 female councillors. Women also now make up one quarter of the Shura Council. *(2 marks, evidence linked from two sources)*

Question	General Marking Instructions for this type of question	Max marks	Specific Marking Instructions for this question
5.	(continued) Candidates may be awarded up to a maximum of **2 marks** for incorporating an evaluation of the reliability of the sources in their explanations although this is not mandatory.		**Evidence that opposes the view ("women now have greater political influence")** • Source A, few elected (4–17) out of 2100. • Source A, local councils have limited powers. • Source A, only 130 000 women, 1.35 million men. • Source A, female candidates cannot directly address male voters. • Source A + B, transport difficulties for female voters. • Source C, Shura Council only has power to propose law, no make it. • Sources B + C, only 30 out of 120 Shura Council members. • Source B, only 978 out of 5938 candidates. • Source B, only 0.8% of seats won by females. **Response 2** Women clearly do not experience equality in Saudi Arabian politics. While it is true that 17 women were elected to council positions, they have very little power. Laws are mac by the King and although 30 women now sit on the Shura Council (out of a total of 120) that is hardly equality. Wome won less than 1% of the council seats and find participation difficult due to the restrictions placed on their movement such as being banned from driving a car. *(3 marks, relevant evidence from all three sources with evaluative comment)* Candidates may also be credited up **two marks** on any comment/analysis of the origin and reliability of the source. • Although Source A is fairly up to date (2015) which increases its usefulness and is from a well-respected source (the BBC) it may be slightly biased in its views as it judges issues from a British point of view. *(2 marks)* • Source A is unreliable as it is adapted. *(1 mark)* • Source A is unreliable as it is adapted. We have no idea how much of this article has been adapted. We also have no idea if this truly reflects the content of the original article. *(2 marks)* • Statistics in Source B are up to date (2015). *(0 marks)* • Statistics in Source B are up to date (2015) and so give a fairly up to date picture of the position of men and wome in Saudi Arabia. *(1 mark)* • Source B comes from several different websites. Some are recent but we don't know exactly which statistics come from which source, calling into question Source B's reliability. *(2 marks)* • Source C is unreliable as it is adapted. We have no idea how much of this article has been adapted. We also have no idea who adapted it therefore we cannot be sure that it accurately reflects the views of the original author. *(2 marks)* • Source C is unreliable as Wikipedia can be edited by its users. *(1 marks)* **Response 3** Overall the statement that women now have greater politica influence in Saudi Arabia is largely accurate. They have been allowed to stand for election and have been appointed to the Shura Council (30 women). This is greater than they had before but is still very little influence compared to men. It is striking that only the King can pass laws. *(2 marks)* *For full marks, candidates **must** make an overall judgment as to the extent of the accuracy of the given statement.*

Acknowledgements

Permission has been sought from all relevant copyright holders and Hodder Gibson is grateful for the use of the following:

Source A: Adapted from http://www.bbc.co.uk/news/uk-scotland-scotland-politics-21954909 © BBC and Cancer Research UK (2015 page 4);

Source B: The graph 'Percentage (%) who smoke in Scotland by economic status (2012)' taken from page 10 of Scotland's People Annual Report: Results from 2012 Scottish Household Survey' (http://www.scotland.gov.uk/publications/2013/08/6973/10) © Crown Copyright. Contains public sector information licensed under the Open Government Licence v3.0. (http://www.nationalarchives.gov.uk/doc/open-government-licence/version/3/) 2015 page 5);

Source C: The graph 'Percentage (%) of 13 and 15 year olds who smoke regularly 1990–2013 and 2014–2018 (projected)' taken from 'ASH Scotland: Young people & tobacco' March 2015 (http://www.ashscotland.org.uk/) © ASH Scotland (2015 page 5);

Source A: Adapted from http://www.bbc.co.uk/news/world-middle-east-35086357 © BBC (2017 page 8);

Source C: Adapted from Wikipedia CC BY-SA 3.0 (https://creativecommons.org/licenses/by-sa/3.0/) 2017 page 9).